W9-CTM-782

GARDENING
IN A
SMALL SPACE

GARDENING
IN A
SMALL
SPACE

LANCE HATTATT

Illustrations by
ELAINE FRANKS

BARNES
&NOBLE
BOOKS
NEW YORK

This edition published by Barnes & Noble Inc.,
by arrangement with Parragon

Produced for Parragon by
Robert Ditchfield Publishers
2003 Barnes & Noble Books

Text and illustrations copyright © Parragon 2001
Photographs copyright © Robert Ditchfield 2001
This edition copyright © Parragon 2001
M 10 9 8 7 6 5 4 3 2 1

The illustrations on pages 56 and 57 are by Brenda Stephenson.

All rights reserved. No part of this book may be used or reproduced in any manner
whatsoever without written permission from the publisher.

ISBN 0-7607-3817-3

A copy of the British Library Cataloguing in Publication
Data is available from the Library.

Typeset by Action Typesetting Ltd, Gloucester
Color origination by Colour Quest Graphic Services Ltd,
London E9
Printed and bound in China

Half Title: The award winning small garden featured on
page 68.

Frontispiece: Mirabel Osler's town garden, described on
page 62.

Opposite: The water feature in 'A Garden of Pots' on page
116.

THIS BOOK aims to show the reader how even a small space can be made into a garden of refuge and charm.

It begins by looking at features and styles that are appropriate to limited areas. The central section then considers in detail eleven gardens. Some of these are very small, but even the larger ones are subdivided into spaces that have been designed on a small scale. These gardens help put the features and styles of the first section into context as well as providing inspiring ideas for those wishing to start a new garden.

The final section deals with planting a small space. Naturally many plants of small size are included but there are also larger subjects which can be kept within bounds by pruning and cutting back and which will become valuable members of the small garden.

SYMBOLS

Where measurements are given, the first is the plant's height followed by its spread. The following symbols are also used in this book:

    ○ = thrives best or only in full sun
    ◑ = thrives best or only in part-shade
    ● = succeeds in full shade
    E = evergreen

Where no sun symbol and no reference to sun or shade is made in the text, it can be assumed that the plant tolerates sun or light shade.

Many plants are poisonous and it must be assumed that no part of a plant should be eaten unless it is known that it is edible.

Contents

Right: A view of the gravel garden
featured on page 92.

Gardening in a Small Space

Increasingly more and more people find themselves gardening in a small space. As land values have soared and house prices spiralled, so the opportunity of owning a large garden becomes less and less. This, together with a move away from the openness of the countryside to the comparative restriction of town and city, has meant a complete reappraisal of gardening technique and style. Coupled to this is a marked change in the use of leisure time where, today, so many extra demands are placed upon the individual that, however willing, there is simply insufficient time and resources available to manage the more spacious gardens of yesterday.

FACING UP TO CHALLENGES

A limited space does, of course, bring with it its own particular challenges, requiring imaginative and flexible management and organizational skills. Gardens which may be seen in their entirety throughout the year in all seasons demand original and innovative ideas if interest is to be maintained at all times. Aesthetics play a major part too, for it is important that the materials and artefacts used in the garden are not simply appropriate, but well suited to their surroundings.

Small gardens inevitably restrict choice. A tiny space, sadly, does not allow for the cultivation of every garden-worthy plant. Nor does it admit all design features anymore than it accommodates every style. Instead, it calls for self-discipline, for the formulation of clear, often simple, solutions and for the ability to work and rework ideas until they present a cohesive, unified whole. But in this lies much of the fun and enjoyment.

Privacy is, understandably, always a consideration. And where the garden becomes a very real, and much used, extension to the indoors, then account should be taken of this at the planning stage. Similarly a balance must be drawn between the garden purely as a place of beauty and somewhere that has an effective, functional purpose. Discrete areas will need to be found for compost, for garbage, for the storing of tools and garden machinery, for fuel, as well as for garden furniture, cold frames, old pots and such similar items.

The small garden must, as a matter of course, be all-purpose. It cannot,

All available space has been artfully utilized here to provide a succession of color lasting right through the summer and into the fall. Note how annuals are mixed with perennials to extend the season of interest.

A small lawn, raised borders and an ancient fruit tree provide the perfect setting for outdoor meals in this tiny city garden.

nor should it, cater for the needs of the gardener alone but should aim to provide for other family members as well. Where there are young children, then a play area with room for a sandpit, swings or climbing frame may be a necessity. For others, a space in which to relax, to entertain friends, to enjoy meals outside, perhaps a barbeque. There may indeed be divided loyalties. Compromises will have to be reached, but it is through these that the garden will adopt its own identity and, ultimately, be in harmony with its owner.

ASSESSING THE SITE

Aspect, the way in which a garden faces, will be of greater significance in a small area. Surrounding buildings, a neighboring tree or trees, or simply the wrong aspect may well result in an overall lack of sunshine. On the other hand, it may be that the site is very open and exposed to the sun and will, accordingly, be hot and dry.

Soil type will be another determining factor in deciding which plants to grow. The degree of alkalinity or acidity of the soil, measured on a pH scale, is an indicator of what will flourish. A pH of 7.0 equals a neutral soil, above is alkaline, below acid. Some plants such as rhododendrons, pieris and summer-flowering heathers, will not tolerate lime and will only succeed on acid soils with a low pH. Others, like bearded irises and peonies, seem to prefer some lime content. Whatever, the vast majority of plants are unfussy and will, if well tended, grow quite happily. Most garden centres sell simple but effective soil testing kits so that it is relatively easy to ascertain soil type with a high degree of accuracy.

Small gardens, which are usually but not always enclosed, create their own micro-climate. The result is that it may be possible to cultivate successfully more of those plants which are generally thought to be on the borderline of hardiness. However, one has to admit that some gardens may well, on account of their situation, be particularly exposed to cold and suffer as frost pockets. Wind chill, as damaging as the sharpest of frosts, is something else to be considered. Very often the gap between buildings, usually quite narrow, forms a wind tunnel exposing anything within its path to winter gusts and gales. Where this is the case it may be necessary to devise some kind of shield or screening to lessen the

A narrow path between buildings, as here, can often form a wind tunnel.

impact of the wind.

CREATING STYLE

Taking over an existing garden is sometimes less easy than beginning from nothing. Do not be afraid to dispense with anything unwanted, the removal of which is practical. Creating an individual style of the garden which is allowed to become a dominant and recurring theme will result in something which not only makes a statement but in so doing presents a picture of unity. What style is chosen will, of course, be a matter of personal choice and taste. It may be that an old-fashioned, cottage garden look, currently popular, will particularly appeal where the emphasis is on an informal mixture of fruit, flowers and vegetables. On the other hand, you may prefer a garden which is severely formal, relying particularly on structure, in the form of clipped hedges and walls, and an eye to symmetry where flowers as such play a secondary rôle. What is important is that the finished garden suggests a distinctive style which is consistent and readily identifiable.

Scale, the ratio by which one object is related to another, is certainly one of the most difficult things to balance correctly when planning the outside. Try to look at everything – garden buildings, hard landscaping, trees, shrubs, perennial plantings – not in isolation but in the ways in which they are in proportion one with another.

Color, one of the most pleasing aspects of any garden, needs to be handled in a small space with the utmost care if a spotty, unco-ordinated look is to be avoided. It may

This garden, awarded a gold medal at the Chelsea Flower Show, demonstrates how much of interest may be fitted into a very small area.

A narrow border tightly filled with, in the main, colorful annuals.

chosen not just for leaf but also for flower, interesting bark and possible fall color. Shrubs to include are those which, in addition to unusual flowers, produce berries at the year's end or which may be evergreen. Both, of course, make excellent hosts for all manner of climbers, not least clematis. Even perennial flowers may have particularly fine foliage to be followed with unusual and dramatic seedheads.

Take advantage of any vertical surfaces to double as supports for climbing plants. Horizontals too, such as the uppermost areas of shrubs, fixed ropes and wires, the very tops of boundary walls and fences, may all be employed as homes to climbers.

Planting need not be confined to traditional borders. Raised beds, forming attractive features in their own right, may be used to accommodate a whole range of plants for which there may otherwise be insufficient space. They are especially good for alpines and those subjects which are in need of sharp drainage. All manner of containers, from terracotta pots and classical urns to troughs and discarded sinks, can be employed either singly or in groups to form attractive, colorful arrangements. An advantage of this kind of gardening is that pots may be set aside, or

well prove wise to restrict colors singly or to similar or contrasting tints and tones of the color wheel. Such application calls for a considerable amount of self-discipline but can produce most worthwhile results. Indeed, form and the texture of foliage, not to mention scent, are as demanding of attention as is the arrangement of flower color.

CREATIVE PLANTING

Where planting is concerned, small gardens concentrate the mind. Focus on those which are reliable, which perform well and which, if possible, contribute interest over an extended period. Trees, for example, may be replanted, once their season of interest has passed. Do not overlook the potential of exterior walls. As well as being clothed in climbers, they may be furnished with hanging pots, baskets or window boxes to lift and brighten what might be dismissed as uninteresting façades.

For those with a spirit of adventure, it is possible to shape any number of evergreens into imaginative works. Yew and box are most commonly used for topiary but holly, shrubby honeysuckles, Portuguese laurel, bay and ivy may all be trimmed and trained successfully and effectively.

Gardening in a small space may, for you, be nothing greater than a few pots displayed on a balcony or window sill. That matters not at all. In fact the smallest gardens ever are those usually to be found at a village fête in summer. Consisting of a seed tray filled with soil they conspire to include a handful of gravel for paths, mossy lawns, twiggy fences and tiny, tiny borders planted out with miniature dianthus and aromatic thymes.

They embody the essential ingredients for any garden anywhere and from observing them, as in closely looking at all gardens everywhere, we may all learn to strive towards that ultimate happiness and contentment which is the reward of all gardening.

Tiny gardens need not, nor should they be, without interest. This one makes excellent use of foliage plants, which convey a sense of plenty.

Patios and Paved Areas

For many people gardening in a really small area a traditional lawn would not only be inappropriate and out of place but also totally impractical. Paving, in one form or another, is an ideal solution allowing access to the garden in all weathers and at all times of year.

Old flagstones, granite sets, cobbles, brick and gravel all make for attractive and interesting hardlandscaping. Where reclaimed brick and stone may prove to be too expensive, a wide range of cheaper materials is readily available. An alternative is to use treated wooden planks as decking.

Reproduction paving stones have been used informally in this patio garden to form a winding path.

Sun streams into this corner where trellis over fencing and a painted arbor unite to trap the heat.

Carefully controlled color is the inspiration behind this randomly paved terraced area which immediately adjoins the house. Frothy lady's mantle, *Alchemilla mollis*, is allowed to seed at will, as are poppies and violas.

A very modern design like this one depends entirely for its success on the bold execution of a relatively simple idea.

Gravel, into which plants are allowed to grow, contrasts with regularly shaped paving to give this modern garden a clear sense of purpose.

Surround a seat, such as this one, with
pots full of summer flowering lilies.
These are excellent for cultivation in
containers where they should be kept
well watered during the growing
season.

Seats in Small Gardens

Of course gardening is about work but it should, equally, be concerned with relaxation. This is especially so of the small garden which so often doubles as an outside room either for sitting or eating outdoors.

Seats in small gardens need to be multi-purpose. On the one hand they must be aesthetically pleasing, to look attractive and inviting and to fit in with their surroundings. On the other hand, they are required to be functional, to fit their purpose, to be robust, weather resistant and long lasting.

Natural or painted wood, metal, stone and plastic are all materials which come to little harm if exposed to the elements.

Although this seat is a perfect resting place, its principal purpose is as a focal point within a small garden.

A well crafted rustic seat which is accommodated into a small alcove set between stone walls. Overhanging shrubs enhance an atmosphere of timelessness.

19

Containers

Pots and containers are an absolute necessity for gardens in very limited spaces. It is tempting to say that there is not anything which cannot be grown in a pot; it is often very surprising what will succeed.

Good drainage is essential if you are to be successful with plants in pots. In containers designed for some other purpose several open drainage holes must be made in the bottom. Over these a layer of crocks, put in before the compost and any planting takes place, will prevent the growing medium from becoming water-logged.

A clever arrangement of window boxes, placed at various heights, and an assortment of pots are home to this colorful display.

Concrete was no obstacle
(see 'A Garden of Pots'
page 116) when it came to
clothing walls.

Hostas are excellent
subjects for pots.

Spring bedding, consisting of bright-eyed pansies and
yellow tulips, looks particularly well in this handsome,
classical urn.

Yet again the ingenuity of the owners of 'A Garden of Pots' (see page 116) is put to the test. The projecting roof of the outhouses forms a shelf upon which are placed a number of colorful pots.

Solanum rantonnetii, a tender climber, is positioned during the summer months at the base of a flight of steps in 'A Gravel Garden' (see page 92).

A pot grown agave forms the centerpiece of this walled courtyard garden which, although enclosed, attracts the sun.

Bay trees lend themselves to being treated as standards. This one has a fine twisted stem.

Santolina, or cotton lavender, flourishes in this large, glazed stoneware pot. In fact this pot would look equally good empty.

A beautifully proportioned, pleasingly decorated jar which is of sufficient size as to be included in this pretty garden.

Mirabel Osler (see page 62) has included this stone pot in her town garden purely as a piece of decoration.

Home-grown strawberries are the very being of
summer and may be cultivated most successfully in a
clay strawberry planter. Even before the ripening of
the fruits the foliage, and then the flower, is appealing.

Nothing could be simpler than this shallow dish filled with various forms of houseleek.

A stone trough has been utilized here to form a miniature scree bed for tiny succulents. The top surface is dressed with horticultural grit.

An entire rock garden, beautifully planted, and all arranged in an antique stone trough. A cerise colored phlox cannot escape notice.

Small-growing varieties of hardy geranium need not be thought unsuitable for growing in a container. A top dressing of grit serves to improve drainage.

A bar running across the window sill provides a built-in support for a collection of pots. Always, of course, ensure that fixings are secure.

Plants packed tightly together guarantee that any display looks purposeful.

The façade of this town house is greatly enlivened with this collection of summer bedding.

Cool whites, creams and blues are included together in this very sophisticated, imaginative and well planted window box.

Another very thoughtful and carefully considered scheme. Here hot reds and purples, some blatantly clashing, are kept in check with fresh green foliage.

Window boxes do not have to be for summer only.

Hanging baskets are huge fun and give scope to all manner of plant combinations. Bought ready prepared, or filled yourself, they will add sparkle to even the dullest of spots. Remember, they require copious amounts of water.

This hanging basket has been prepared with spring in mind.

A plain brick wall becomes the focus of attention with this basket.

Fuchsia 'Miss California' is of the softest of pinks.

Paths

In the majority of gardens paths represent one of the major aspects of hard land-scaping. Materials from which they may be formed are many and varied. The final choice will depend largely on the purpose of the path, its situation and frequency of use. Old flagstones or bricks, laid in a variety of patterns, always look good but are, sadly, expensive. Gravel is a very much cheaper substitute but needs to be contained within an edging. Cobbles and granite sets look very effective and are now readily available as modern reproductions. Cinder or bark paths are ideally suited to any informal situation.

Within a small space, such as this little enclosed garden, the path takes on an important rôle. Serving two functions, it is intended both for decoration as well as for access.

Here a series of flagstones is set at intervals through a border, the gaps carpeted with acaena.

A sympathetic treatment of a path for a herb garden which makes imaginative use of reclaimed materials.

The whole of this garden has been shaped by the positioning of paths and steps. Materials are the same for both in order to give a feeling of unity in what is, after all, a small area.

Changes of Level

Steps in any garden, however small, and whether by design or through necessity, invite an immediate response. Here is a different area to be explored, there a change of mood. Climb up and there is a sense of achievement, of reaching a goal. Descend and the way is unknown, fully of mystery and excitement.

Construction may be of the simplest. A few timbers set as risers into a sloping site, the treads of compacted earth, will, in the right situation, be as appropriate as is a flight of stone steps complete with balustrade elsewhere. Straight flights of cut stone are best reserved for where you intend formality. Narrow, twisting steps fit better into an informal, more relaxed garden.

Good quality engineering bricks have been used as the basis for this short flight of steps leading from the garden to the terrace.

This broad flight of steps is one of the main points of interest of 'A Gravel Garden' (see page 92). Tiny plants have been encouraged to fill the cracks.

These steps, wide at the top approach, draw the visitor down from the upper level.

Simply constructed, yet completely practical, these steps make use of rough sawn timbers.

Elegant stairs, complete with iron railings, mark the entrance to this town house. The boundary has been planted out with a series of boxes.

Water Features

Water in a garden is particularly appealing. Whether as a small, trickling stream, or as a formal pool or as a natural pond, it is bound to excite interest. Placing a water feature within a large garden presents few problems. In a small space the choice becomes much more limited and care has to be exercised to see that everything remains in scale.

Today with the availability of all manner of electric pumps for fountains and spouts, with preformed streams and ponds, with liners available in all sizes, it is possible to find something which is suited to the tiniest of gardens. Even a small pot water feature, surrounded by pebbles and with a small pump recycling water from a hidden bowl, will enliven the garden with its splash or spray.

Before coming to any decision, visit a water garden specialist.

The edges of this small pond are completely masked with generous plantings of marginal perennials.

Even the tiniest of gardens need not be without water. This ivy edged pool and fountain belong in 'A Green Town Garden' (see page 88).

A tranquil oasis has been created in this city garden where a formal pool becomes a dominant feature. An emphasis on green contributes to the cool, calm atmosphere.

Very much a rock pool, the construction of this feature makes extensive use of natural stone which has been carefully laid to suggest a natural outcrop.

This kidney-shaped garden pool incorporates a tiny stream and waterfall, the running water helping to keep the surface clear. Large, flat stones form an edge and merge successfully into the rockery on the far side.

Springtime and the rock garden comes into its own. This is the season of the year when so many alpines and rockery plants give of their best. The arrangement of this rock garden is particularly effective for it allows for the inclusion of a tiny stream as well as a small fountain.

These water lilies float contentedly on the surface of an old metal basin removed from a scrapyard.

Designed as a round, this pond fits happily into the top terrace of 'Terracing a Hillside' (see page 96).

'A Garden Designer's Garden' (see page 78) is home to this circular pond which, in turn, is home to a family of goldfish.

An arrangement of mask and container brings that wonderful, musical sound of running water.

This inspired and fascinating water feature provides a cooling effect on a hot summer's day. A submersible pump, placed in a tank below the millstone, allows for the water to be recycled.

A pot fountain surrounded by carefully placed stones and larger rocks is a delightful addition to the corner of this small town garden.

Colorful Bedding

For sheer brilliance of flower color, nothing can compare with the exuberance of massed bedding where the brightest of oranges, yellows and reds vie with each other for attention and position. This is not gardening for the faint hearted but for those who want to enliven a dull space, to bring cheer to the darkest of days and who wish always to be reminded of long, hot sunny hours.

Bedding out need not be confined only to summer. Winter flowering pansies will bloom continuously over the coldest period to be replaced in spring with a wonderful mixture of annuals and bulbs. Indeed, it should be possible to have color in the garden for the majority of the year.

Vibrant Siberian wallflowers interplanted with scarlet tulips are one of the mainstays of this spring bedding scheme.

Here the owners of this small garden have mixed together marigolds, salvias and verbena edged with silver-leafed cineraria.

This path has been giving a daring, colorful treatment. Ribbons of shocking red salvias are interplanted with petunias in shades of magenta, pale mauve and pink. Dwarf, slow growing conifers will, in future years, contribute height.

Tiny though this garden is, it has been given very definite character with this purposeful bedding scheme.

Petunias are a marvelous standby and look so good when, as here, similar shades and tones are massed together.

A Garden of Perennials

Many gardeners, usually because of a lack of time, do not want to be bothered with constantly arranging and rearranging their gardens, often two or three times a year, with annuals, biennials or half hardy plants. For them the answer lies in a garden of perennials where effects, even if varying from season to season, will be constant from one year's end to the next.

Trees, shrubs and herbaceous perennials all fit this category and will, if sensibly chosen, provide year-round interest and demand the minimum of maintenance. In the main work may be regulated to fit in with the individual's life style.

This corner of 'A Concealed Garden' (see page 108) demonstrates how perennial plantings may reduce work to an absolute minimum. Closely planted bugle carpets the ground and effectively smothers weeds.

Deep purple, silver and acidic green form a planting scheme which relies for its effect on foliage.

Beautifully color co-ordinated herbaceous perennials mass this small border for maximum impact.

Here the majority of space has been given over to the creation of a number of tiny borders, each one crammed with perennials.

Most of these plants will be cut back close to ground level in the fall.

The Cottage Garden Look

Cottage gardens are never out of fashion. Perhaps deep down everyone's ideal is to garden in the deepest countryside surrounded by a medley of old fashioned flowers, home grown produce, meandering streams and sun-dappled grass. It is, therefore, hardly surprising that there is, in cities, suburbs and rural areas alike, so much interest in the cottage garden look.

A small garden is no bar to the cottage garden look. Even within a quite tiny space it is still possible to create the kind of delightful chaotic profusion which is so much admired. Well chosen perennials, a scattering of annual seed, scented shrubs, perhaps a miniature pond, and you should achieve a garden which rapidly becomes a haven from the modern world.

Self-sown foxgloves, *Digitalis purpurea*, intermingle with *Knautia macedonica*. The spherical head of the allium reflects the euphorbia.

This is very much in the tradition of the cottage garden where flower mixes with fruit.

An enchanting border mixture made up of a deep pink rose, a similar colored diascia and all surrounded by a carpet of the white viola, *Viola cornuta alba*. This is cottage gardening with subtle sophistication which in no way detracts from its original purpose.

Small City Gardens

If, as many of us do, you live in a large town or city, then it is very unlikely that you will have much space for a garden of any size.

In the main, the smaller the area the simpler the basic idea should be. More of less works well in most garden situations and, when applied to tiny spaces, some stunning effects may be achieved. Form and texture may well be as important as color which, for the most part, is seasonal and not always easy to maintain. Green, as a color, is important in a heavily built-up area for it is suggestive of the countryside which lies beyond the town.

Much of the appeal of this city front garden lies in the fact that it has been planted for year-round interest. Evergreens, such as elaeagnus, skimmia and aucuba, ensure that there is something to look at even in the depths of winter.

The simple, quiet charm of this small court is maintained by dense plantings of evergreen shrubs and climbers.

An unusual boat-shaped border in which color is mainly limited to white with an accent of blue.

Evergreens, principally in tones of silver and green, make a welcoming statement at the entrance to this town house.

Magnolia 'Leonard Messel' flanked by scented choisya are the key plantings in this easily maintained, paved court.

The Kitchen Garden

Where space is at a real premium, then establish a kitchen garden in a series of pots. It is quite surprising the number of vegetables which may be grown successfully under these conditions. Herbs, too, thrive in containers and may even be kept in the light on a kitchen window sill.

Vegetables and herbs do not have to be relegated to plots away from the flower garden. Many are not without decorative qualities and may be fitted snugly amongst shrubs and perennials where they will mature in an unobtrusive manner. Indeed, many traditional herbs are grown in mixed borders as a matter of course. Runner beans, always a favorite, take up very little space when grown up a wigwam sited at the back of the border.

Even the smallest of kitchen gardens can be exceedingly productive when crops are planted closely.

The way to the back gate is set out with a pleasant mixture of herbs and perennial flowers. Chinese onions, marjoram, thyme, sage and mint are all but a short step from the kitchen door.

This vegetable border has been subdivided into a number of tiny plots by a series of narrow brick paths. Each area may be serviced without stepping onto and compacting the ground. The rotation of crops becomes easy in this situation.

Neatly trimmed box hedges contain both vegetables and herbs in this decorative potager. Access is via small paths, one brick in width, which follow the line of the hedges. Within each bed are crammed many different crop varieties.

As so many dishes make use of onions it makes good sense to grow your own. This small onion bed is also home to the self-seeding *Viola labradorica*.

The foliage of the onions above has been turned over to expose them to the sun. Soon they will be ready to lift, dry off and store.

This little, neatly edged plot of lettuces would not look out of place anywhere. Easily grown from seed, lettuces will reach maturity within a few weeks. Different varieties have been included here to make summer salads both colorful and interesting.

Asparagus is an absolute luxury. Asparagus crowns, purchased and planted out in spring, require a sunny position in humus rich soil which is well drained. Cropping should not begin until plants are at least three years old. In this instance the asparagus has been interplanted with lettuces to maximize space.

Potatoes need not take up much space. It is possible simply to plant a couple of tubers, concealed somewhere at the back of the border, to enjoy a very satisfying crop. Even an old bucket, given drainage holes, will produce more than satisfactory results.

Carrots, peas, radishes, spinach, spring onions and corn are all very easy vegetables to grow, are decorative in appearance and, most importantly, utilize little in the way of garden space. Each, too, has the further merit of reaching maturity in a relatively short period of time. Because of this valuable ground is not occupied for too long.

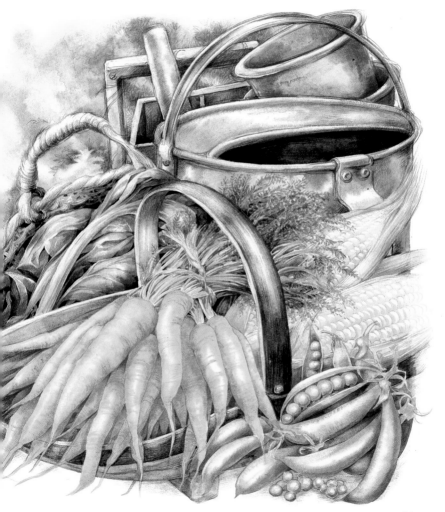

Anyone could adopt this splendid, original idea for growing zucchini. Here a large pot has been given good drainage, filled with fertile soil, planted out and placed in an old chimney pot.

Outdoor tomatoes may easily be grown, as here, in a pot. A sturdy cane to support the trusses, a position in full sun to assist ripening and plenty of water will result in excellent crops. Alternatively they may be cultivated in bags containing an appropriate growing medium. Such bags are sold at most garden centers.

This vegetable plot is so small that even the wheelbarrow has been put to use as a container for the cultivation of zucchini.

Virtually any outside space, however small, could accommodate these runner beans grown in an attractive terracotta pot. As may be seen, even when root growth is restricted there are still more than enough flowers and beans.

Always remember when positioning any container to bear in mind its potential weight when the soil or compost is thoroughly wet.

Ginger mint, *Mentha* x *gentilis*, is fun to grow as an extra special ingredient in a mixed salad dressed with olive oil, vinegar and honey.

A good sized pot, such as this attractive terracotta herb pot, may be planted up with a selection of culinary herbs chosen for their appealing foliage as well as their contribution to the kitchen.

A nicely shaped rosemary and parsley, chives, oregano, French tarragon, winter savory and sage are all suitable for inclusion.

Garden mint, lovely for freshly made mint sauce and jelly, is kept within bounds by being planted in a pot.

The whole of this very flourishing herb garden which, amazingly, is entirely contained within a series of pots, occupies very little space indeed.

One practical aspect of this kind of arrangement is that as plants go over the pots may be removed and replaced with something new and fresh.

Given a layer of gravel above drainage holes, easily drilled into the base, there is no reason at all why almost any container should not be transformed into a miniature herb garden.

With the introduction in recent years of dwarfing and semi-dwarfing rootstocks, it has become increasingly possible for every gardener to enjoy the pleasurable experience of plucking ripe fruit straight from the tree.

Where space is very much at a premium, then fruit trees may be trained against walls, fences or on wires in the form of cordons, espaliers or fans.

In situations where there is only room for a single tree, then it must, naturally, be a self-fertile variety.

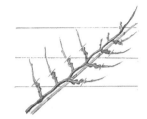

FORMING A CORDON

Following the planting of a feathered maiden, reduce all sideshoots over 4in/10cm long to three buds. The leader should remain unpruned.

The time to begin summer pruning of established cordons is once shoots have developed woody bases.

Shorten laterals to three leaves and sub-laterals to one leaf beyond the basal cluster. Shorten the leader to 6in/15cm above the top wire.

Step-over apples, like these, are an excellent answer to the problem of growing fruit in a very small garden. Plant along the edge of a border, or at the side of a path.

FORMING AN ESPALIER

1. Prune a maiden tree back to a good bud 2in /5cm above the first wire.

2. In summer train the leading shoot to a cane. Train two side branches to canes. Shorten other sideshoots to three leaves.

A well-established espalier apple tree. During the mid to late summer laterals should be shortened back to three leaves and sub-laterals to one.

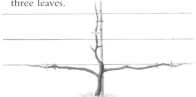

3. In late fall tie down the first tier. Prune the leader to a bud, just above the second wire. Shorten other sideshoots to three buds.

4. In subsequent summers train the leader vertically and the two lateral branches at 45°. Shorten all other sideshoots to three leaves. Prune back the leader in winter.

Gooseberries need not, as might previously be thought, only be grown on bushes. In this imaginative scheme they have been trained along wires fixed to the house wall where, in full sunshine, they crop well.

This gooseberry bush has been grown as a standard to form a centerpiece to one of the sections of this box-edged kitchen garden.

Grapevines are, it is true, vigorous growers and will, in a normal situation, take up a great deal of space and certainly more than can be afforded in the small garden. However, with strict training they may be grown as cordons or espaliers or accommodated over arbors, arches or pergolas.

A strawberry jar will allow fruit to develop without the risk of becoming muddied by earth. Place in full sun and keep well watered for fruit to ripen.

Currants need not be confined to particular areas for they merge quite happily into mixed borders.

Selected Gardens

The gardens in this section are very individual. Some require a high degree of maintenance, others comparatively little; some are very colorful, others rely more on shape and texture for their appeal.

A Garden Writer's Garden

Mirabel Osler's town garden, measuring little more than 70 x 30ft/21 x 9m, is a garden of extraordinary style. Underlying the whole garden is a strong framework of walls, paths, steps, interesting structures, unusual topiary, strategically placed containers and seats. Against this background is a wealth of planting where great emphasis is placed on foliage rather than flower. Color, beyond all shades and tones of green, is deliberately restricted and controlled.

Everywhere space is used in a thoughtful and imaginative manner. This is illustrated in the ways in which the boundaries have been completely concealed, utilities, such as a potting shed, accommodated, a water feature included, and a number of tiny but distinctly separate enclosures, each serving a definite purpose, have been woven into the whole.

Concealed mirrors not only reflect light but suggest the surreal.

A solitary chair captures the sun's rays and invites a moment's pause and reflection. Although very much a town garden, there is a wonderful sense of privacy, of the world at a distance, of harmony with nature.

Framed by a plain but attractive wooden arch (opposite), a stone and brick path, the principal axis of the garden, draws the eye towards the distant boundary where a door, set in the wall, invites exploration of the beyond. That the door is false, and leads to nowhere, simply serves to highlight the imaginative detail which is to be found throughout this garden. A nice touch is the way in which at the lower level of the path the diamond shapes are of stone on brick. This pattern is reversed up the steps.

A beautifully planned sitting out area for summer meals. Clipped box encloses this outdoor room whilst *Salix caprea* 'Kilmarnock', the Kilmarnock willow, has, unusually, been shaped into lollipops. Behind the bench seat mirrors are placed; these effectively give an illusion of space.

A raised border gives necessary drainage to a collection of sun-loving plants, amongst which helianthemum (rock roses) are encouraged to tumble down the face of the stone wall.

Within the gravel garden a sculpted slate urn is the dominant feature. Once more a mirror is used for an on-going reflection. Here the fastigiate yew is employed as a support for a climbing rose whose twining stems, ingeniously, assist in keeping the evergreen in shape.

This little water feature is conveniently placed to sink a can for summer watering.

Placed where it may be reflected in a mirror, a wicker basket for the collection of prunings and other garden waste.

These few shallow steps leading to the false door terminate a main vista. A pair of empty urns contribute symmetry.

Trapped by the heat of the sun, this generous grouping of pots conjures up the spirit of the Mediterranean.

Returning to the house, attention focuses on an arrangement of pots placed beside the open door. Plants are encouraged to spill over from the borders.

Incredibly this charming summerhouse is tucked away into a tiny space just off the main path. Carefully sited, it is positioned to look directly across the gravel garden where, artfully, a visual color link is made.

Paint is important in this garden. Here the exterior of the summerhouse is painted grey-blue with details picked out in grey-green. Within, a bench seat, useful for storage purposes, is colored a wonderful, distressed chalk-blue, a color repeated on some of the wood panels behind. These in turn are set off with alternate panels of pale terracotta.

Gardens are, very naturally, not only places in which to work but are also, as indicated here, places of leisure.

An Award Winning Small Garden

Considerable skill and ingenuity on the owners' part have gone into the creation and maintenance of this colorful edge-of-town garden.

What is incredible, and wholly impressive, is that the vast majority of all the plants are raised by the owners in their small, standard greenhouse which, later in the year, becomes a principal attraction in its own right.

Early spring and the greenhouse is just getting under way. Young seedlings, neatly pricked out, are starting to take root.

Cheerful daffodils, polyanthus and yellow-flowered forsythia contribute early spring color. Cold frames are already fully utilized with stock being brought on for the main flowering season which, pictured right, occurs in summertime.

68

By early summer the garden is taking on a very different appearance. Both borders and pots are starting to burgeon.

Compared with the start of the gardening year, the greenhouse is set to come into its own.

Herbaceous perennials cram the border. Here are to be found lupins, delphiniums, clematis, roses, lilies and scarlet *Lychnis chalcedonica*.

Midsummer and the garden is a riot of many splendid hues, each jostling for position and attention. All the hard work, and no little anxiety, of the early year come to fruition in this cavalcade of color.

By now the interior of the greenhouse is full to bursting point.

Staging, arranged in tiers, is essential to display this many plants to such good effect.

Large numbers of the plants used in the summer displays, such as these elegant fuchsias, are not able to withstand low winter temperatures. Protection from frost, in a heated greenhouse, is essential for their survival.

Fuchsias, some tender, some hardy, are amongst the mainstays of the summer bedding.

Bright heads of begonias provide startling color as the season progresses.

A narrow bed against the garage wall is home to massed planting. Edging the grass is a row of pink and red geranium, their felted, marked leaves providing additional interest.

Planting in and around the patio makes use of soft pinks, white, violet-blue and deep purple.

A flourish of color descends the house wall in the form of a swag of flowers.

A Family Town Garden

A grass path of generous proportions runs from the house to the far boundary. Mellow brick walls give shelter to an attractive mix of plants.

Creating a garden which is, on the one hand, inviting and accessible to young children and, on the other, retains a sense of order and purpose, and is in itself a visual delight, is no easy matter. But that is exactly what has been achieved in this stylish small garden which lies behind a Georgian town house.

For the gardener, this is a flower garden of the utmost charm. Traditional borders of trees, shrubs and herbaceous perennials are combined with a sunny terraced area, shady corner and places for sitting.

Surrounded by self-seeded foxgloves, this bench seat is a pleasant place in which to absorb the sights, sounds and scents of the garden.

What child could resist the thrill of this proper tree house? Purpose built, and approached by a stout ladder, this is something straight from the pages of Peter Pan.

This corner of a border (left) conveys a wonderful sense of plants in profusion. Here are to be found everyone's favorites set out in daring abandon. Delphiniums, lupins, columbines and forget-me-nots are joined by cistus, irises and roses. This is the cottage garden of the past reborn into the town. In short, plants are given free-reign and they respond well.

In direct contrast to the more open borders, this area of shade captures an entirely different mood. Greater emphasis is placed on foliage and form, less on color. Here is something altogether quieter, more subdued, a retreat from the bright sunlight which floods the other end of the garden.

A brick terrace running alongside the house ends in a plethora of foliage. Much thought has been given to the placing of different shrubs, grasses and ferns to create a tapestry of green.

Summer meals are enjoyed in this sunny, open-air dining area which, situated close to the back door, is convenient for the kitchen. On the wall an arrangement of ceramic tiles forms an outdoor picture.

A Garden Designer's Garden

Jacquie Gordon, a garden designer, was faced with the challenge of creating a private space within an area overlooked by a new housing development. One of the main priorities was, understandably, to provide complete seclusion yet maintain a degree of openness.

As someone with a demanding career, consideration needed to be given to the amount of time available for maintenance. If the garden were to fit in with a busy lifestyle, then it had to be capable for the most part of looking after itself.

The garden as it was. An ugly fence, barely concealed, the windows of neighboring houses.

Contrasts of form and texture are the keynote here. A giant phormium, whose spiky leaves stab at the skyline, is balanced by a feathery acer.

It is scarcely possible that this (see opposite) is the same garden. No longer overlooked, unsightly fencing obliterated, all to be replaced by a tapestry of plants, thoughtfully positioned hard landscaping and a seemingly casual arrangement of pots and containers.

Blocking out a view which lacks interest, this planting of trees adds necessary height and depth to the end of the garden.

This grouping of pots, almost a pot garden in itself, brings color and interest to this corner of the garden.

No garden should be without a seating area. Here daring paint colors of slate-blue and fabrics of cerise pink have been used to great effect.

A bird's eye view of the entire garden. From the vantage point of an upstairs window it is possible to appreciate fully the design, structure and plantings of this most intriguing garden.

Circles, suggested in the pool, the many plant containers and the shape of the border, are in marked contrast to the angular paving, the bamboo screen, even the bench. Vertical accents are reinforced by the trunks of the trees, tall growing perennials, among them stately euphorbias, and the old chimney pot, now invested with a new lease of life as a plant pot holder.

A Plant Lover's Garden

In dividing up a fairly typical back garden in a leafy suburb of a small cathedral city, the owners deliberately set out to create two very distinct and special areas for rare and beautiful plants. Neither space is at all large, but this has proved no barrier to creating borders designed for year-round interest.

Gardening in this way is both time consuming and labor intensive. Spring flowering bulbs are removed as they go over, their spaces filled with unusual summer bedding. Perennials, if they are to be kept in peak condition, must be lifted and divided on a regular basis. Excessive growth on trees and shrubs is constantly checked to maintain a correct balance within borders. Climbers are tied-in and trained in accordance with a master plan. All of this beside the routine tasks of dead-heading, of lawn care, of weeding and feeding, of mulching and, when necessary, watering.

Pastel shades of early summer dominate a well structured herbaceous border. Close planting not only ensures that a maximum number of plants may be fitted into a small space, but minimises the need for staking.

Majestic delphiniums, Pacific Hybrids, contrast wonderfully with a deep background of a plum colored prunus. Cut down once the flower spires are finished, they will in all probability reward with a repeat flowering.

Parallel herbaceous borders in the grand manner have been adapted to a small space. Linked by similar but not identical plantings, they terminate in an inviting arbor wreathed in honeysuckle, *Lonicera × americana*, and the sweetly scented rose, *Rosa* 'New Dawn'.

A paved path (left), provides a colorful link between the two garden areas. Pots of white marguerites, beautifully cool and summery, unify both sides. In the foreground the half-hardy geranium, *Geranium malviflorum*, sprays out onto the flags.

From the seat in the arbor the vista is closed by this formal arrangement set before a tightly clipped privet hedge. Shaped box, grown in sturdy terracotta pots, guard a handsome plinth and ball made from salvaged materials.

Surrounding the plinth (right) is a massed planting of the crimson thistle, *Cirsium rivulare* 'Atropurpureum'. This perennial requires an open, sunny spot where it will flower for many weeks on end.

Rain contributes a soft, slightly melancholy air to this approach to the white garden. Across the rose arch, *Rosa* 'Albéric Barbier' and *Rosa* 'Alister Stella Gray' tussle for position.

Gravel, at the center of which a stone bird bath forms a focal point, encourages self-seeding which contributes an air of relaxation in an otherwise formal setting.

One of the main achievements of this garden comes from the way in which the owners have handled changes of direction and mood. Movement from one area to another, from one color scheme to another, is gradual.

A Green Town Garden

Few, if any, could fail to be captivated by the utter charm of this, the most delightful of tiny, tiny town gardens. Approached from the busy street through a handsome brick arch, this oasis of green offers a haven of order, peace and tranquillity in direct contrast to the commotion of modern day life to be found outside its walls.

In describing it as a green garden is not, of course, to suggest that all plantings are restricted to this one color. But what the owners have done in the first instance is to build up a background and structure of foliage plants, chosen for form and texture, against which to set off carefully selected flowering shrubs and perennials. Planting within a very small space demands great discipline.

A garden such as this is not necessarily low on maintenance. Fewer flowers there may be, but a program of regular pruning, training and trimming is required to ensure that nature is kept within bounds.

Looking from the street towards the house (above), the edges of the pathway are crammed with an exciting mixture of plants. Punctuating the path are a series of evergreen *Chamaecyparis lawsoniana* 'Columnaris'.

The view (opposite) from the house. On the left a plinth of small leafed ivy is surmounted by a terracotta pot containing box. Midway towards the entrance the white bark of *Betula utilis* var. *jacquemontii* soars upwards.

From the conservatory a path, flanked by two splendid stone dogs, invites exploration of a second garden area. The way in which the path is designed to curve slightly has the effect of appearing to lengthen the distance as well as preventing the whole from being seen at a glance. Planting is wonderfully dense and varied, chosen to give depth and intensity to a small space. A number of different ivies used as ground cover also act to soften stone edges.

Raised beds have been used widely throughout this garden. Retaining stone walls have the effect of sinking paths to a lower level and allowing them to take on an intimacy otherwise denied.

As the way gently curves to rejoin the path at the front of the house, so the eye is drawn once more to another quiet but inspiring planting scheme. Here green is highlighted with white. Tall growing white foxgloves, *Digitalis purpurea albiflora*, combine with the masterwort, *Astrantia major involucrata*, to float among a dappled canopy of leaves.

A Gravel Garden

A flight of stone steps leads from the house down into this gravel garden. Enclosed on all sides by high walls, the heat from the summer sun remains trapped so that the entire court enjoys a very favorable micro-climate.

A thick mulch of pea gravel acts as an irregular path through the garden. In practical terms this not only reflects the heat but also serves to conserve moisture. Additionally, of course, the gravel provides sun-loving plants with the sharp drainage that they require if they are to thrive.

Planting is very much color-themed. Soft pinks, lilacs, lavenders and mauves are highlighted with a touch of crimson, isolated instances of indigo blue and splashes of palest lemon. Glaucous foliage, typical of plants capable of withstanding the hot sun, contributes to the overall effect. A changing display of pots guarantees that the garden is never static.

Lovely combinations such as this one may be achieved by pairing plants. Pictured here are *Wisteria floribunda* and *Clematis montana* 'Tetrarose'.

Finely divided leaves of *Choisya ternata* 'Aztec Pearl' give this Mexican orange bush a particular appeal. Blue camassias complete the picture.

This splendid, glazed Ali Baba pot is home to a fine specimen of *Aeonium arboreum*.

Dierama enjoys the good drainage of the gravel garden.

Frequent pruning is necessary to check the growth of *Hippophaë rhamnoïdes* included as a foil to *Rosa* 'Cerise Bouquet'.

Large clumps of the low-growing, pretty pink *Phuopsis stylosa* are encouraged to sprawl at the edge of the gravel.

All of the cistus love to be baked so their inclusion in this hot, dry garden is of little surprise. *Cistus* 'Elma', shown here, has been chosen for its large, papery-white petals surrounding a centre of golden stamens.

Flowers of *Cistus* 'Peggy Sammons' intermingle in this scheme with the lilac trumpets of *Penstemon glaber*. Regular dead-heading of the penstemon keeps flower color all summer long.

Terracing a Hillside

Situated in an enviable position on the edge of a major city overlooking a deep gorge, the steepness of the site of this garden called for radical treatment. Julian Dowle, international garden designer, decided, in consultation with the owner, to reconstruct and redesign the series of small terraces linked by steps and meandering paths. Coupled with this he arranged for a number of formal and informal pools, connected by water courses and channels, to form a principal feature of the garden as a whole.

The result is a garden or, more accurately, several individual gardens, which have been designed to take full advantage of spectacular views, which harmonize with the surrounding landscape.

Beyond the fine view, glimpsed through overgrown trees, there is little to commend the garden as it was.

Hard landscaping is in place and the garden is beginning to take shape as a series of linked terraces.

Looking upwards towards the house the extent of the terracing is immediately apparent. At this stage planting is yet to be undertaken.

Lush planting (below) successfully masks the somewhat stark edges of the hard landscaping and gives to the whole garden a slight air of mystery.

An informally shaped pool is the
dominant feature of this level. Close
planting includes many moisture loving
marginals.

Extensive use is made of hostas and
bergenias, their broad leaves associating
well with water.

Contrasts of form and texture are
achieved in this imaginative poolside
planting.

Here you are able to be at eye-level with
this pool of water. An utterly magical
experience.

The gazebo sits snugly in the corner of two walls on this lower level. Sides are clothed with climbers.

Water, from an upper reach, cascades down this shute into a formal basin, its splashing sound enjoyed from the seat within the gazebo.

An integral part of an ingenious water system, this lion mask spouts water downwards into the formal pool whilst the fountain returns it up.

A formal pool, complete with fountain, is the keynote of this lower terrace.

Yet another level. Viewed from above, the planting is deliberately restricted so that foliage succeeds flower.

This quiet terrace acts as an interlude before the final way down. An established lime tree gives a canopy of light shade and enhances a cool and restful scheme.

The bottom pool is surrounded with dense plantings. Ferns, goat's beard (*Aruncus dioicus*), marsh marigolds, variegated irises and the paddle leaves of *Lysichiton camtschatcensis* all jostle for position.

A doorway, set into the stone wall, leads out of the garden and gives direct access to the gorge.

Not surprisingly this final garden includes a charming little summerhouse.

The scale of the terracing is quite daunting when viewed from the bottom level. However, cleverly designed breaks together with sympathetic plantings ensure that the stone is never allowed to overpower.

An overall view of the garden. Much of the success of this garden lies in a bold plan supported by well-defined structures against which is a profusion of planting.

An Enclosed Court

High hornbeam hedges completely enclose this small court immediately outside the kitchen door. Old flagstones cover the ground upon which are set a selection of clay pots which are changed according to the season.

For the owners this is a garden in which to relax, to entertain friends and to enjoy the occasional summer meal outside. Because of this low maintenance is a priority but at the same time there is a desire to be surrounded with interesting, unusual and attractive plants.

Scented lilies (see right) are a must for high summer and are especially good as pot specimens. Surrounding these are tender fuchsias, geraniums and well grown eucomis with deep green, strap-like leaves and amazing flower heads.

A lovely combination of *Lilium* 'Pink Perfection', fuchsia and dainty nemesia.

Dark headed fuchsias are a perfect foil for the shell-pink bells of pot grown *Azorina vidalii*.

Wonderful waxy blooms of *Kirengeshoma palmata* are cultivated in a narrow border where they enjoy the partially shady situation. These later flowering perennials are not difficult to grow but should be given humus-rich soil which is kept moist during the flowering period.

Close to the kitchen door (left) is a fine example of the winter flowering *Garrya elliptica*.

Clear pink blooms of
Camellia 'Anticipation' are
teamed up here with the
darker tones of the spring
flowering *Clematis alpina*
'Ruby'.

Clipped box edges the
borders which surround
this courtyard garden
(right). Plumes of *Smilacina
racemosa* complete the
spring picture.

A Concealed Garden

Nothing in the approach, through the sprawling suburbs of a large industrial city, prepares the visitor for the unique quality of this totally secret and superbly styled garden. To pass through the gates is to enter a world transformed. Gone is the bleakness of the outer suburbs to be replaced with a garden, though small in overall size, which has been cleverly crafted into a series of outside rooms.

Immediately it is apparent that form and structure mean a great deal to the owners. Clipped yew hedging is used on a grand scale as the principal means of delineating enclosures. Box is fashioned in balls, cones, pyramids and spirals, or simply used as low divisions, to give unity, and a sense of fun, to individual areas. Recycled timbers give substance to paths and steps, strongly countering any suggestion of the whimsy.

For although much use is made of flowering shrubs and perennials, this is not in essence a flower garden. The passion here is for symmetry, for proportion, shape and order.

As busy professional people, the owners are able to give less time than they would like to garden maintenance. To this end the garden has been planned to survive and yet to look good for long periods of time.

A cross vista, terminating in a sculptural shell, is strongly defined with a series of box cones. Paths are of gravel contained within granite sets which are in keeping with an overall severity of style.

Bold steps framed with hefty wooden stumps are almost in themselves an item of sculpture. The uncompromising, rather masculine mood of the garden is softened with carefully thought out plantings.

This cross path, opening onto an expanse of grass, has been planned deliberately to be narrow in order to create spatial contrast.

Formal structures and informal plantings go hand in hand in this simple but effective area. A pair of stone vases contain a mixture of houseleeks.

Unashamedly theatrical, this dramatic flight of outdoor stairs rises towards a stark, elemental sculpture.

Tightly clipped box balls demonstrate the importance that the owners of this garden give to form. A nice touch has been to imitate the shape of the box with the heads of ornamental onions, just now going to seed.

Framed on all sides by hedges of yew, this boldly painted seat acts both as a focal point to end a vista and also as a resting place.

House colors are applied in this situation where the bench seat becomes part of a much larger composition.

One of the underlying strengths of this garden is the way in which it is possible to look from one enclosure into another.

In order for it to be effective box hedging must be kept crisply cut at all times.

This side of the silver and white garden is dominated by a summerhouse faced in dressed stone.

The fourth approach, as seen from the summerhouse, takes good account of perspective.

Four weeping ash (above) dominate this grassy enclosure which, in atmosphere, is reminiscent of the shady area so often to be found in the center of a southern French town.

This handsome door (left), which is in fact leading nowhere, succeeds in turning a dead end into a point of interest.

Placed in front of the door is this most intriguing box square (below).

Here (above) box hedging is angled to the descent of the steps to give them a neat and definitive edge.

Box spirals like this one (right) require a great deal of time and patience in the making before they achieve the desired effect.

Looking back towards the entrance to the garden, the way in which the whole is designed to be totally concealed becomes apparent. The gateway lies in fact on the right, approached through the curtains of yew.

A Garden of Pots

Incredible as it may at first appear, this garden is completely made up of plants grown in pots and containers. Realizing that the area available to them did not permit a garden in the traditional sense, the owners opted to satisfy their love of foliage and flowers by growing them in an ingenious and highly individual manner.

Gardening like this is not without its problems. Watering must be carried out regularly. A program of systematic feeding is also necessary.

This fine, well established hedge gives all the appearance of having been in place for many, many years. It is grown in old tubs.

Room has been found to create this relaxed sitting out area where predominantly foliage plants contribute to an overall restful atmosphere.

Few people would give more than passing thought to the idea, let alone possibility, of growing Irish yews in pots. And yet these splendid examples are well and truly contained.

Summer flowering geraniums bring the house alive (above) with an abundance of color during the hottest months of the year.

Both outhouses and garage are framed by the tall growing yew trees (left) which provide a vertical accent within a small area. Even the roof space has been utilized to the full with an imaginative selection of small growing conifers and ivies.

A bewildering array of pots and all manner of containers make up the main part of the garden approached to the right of the entrance. This is pot gardening on a grand scale.

Stout, nicely weathered pots grow beautifully bushy box plants which act within the garden as dividers.

A charmingly positioned water spout surrounded by lush plantings chosen for their variation in texture and form.

Planting a Small Space

This can be the most difficult part of coping with a small garden but even fairly large plants can be accommodated if you know how to control them. Which plants you choose will also determine the style of your garden.

Trees for Height and Interest

Of course we should all like to grow trees. Few gardeners anywhere can fail to be impressed by the sight of majestic oaks studding a landscape park.

Happily there are many small-scale trees, both deciduous and evergreen. In incorporating them into the design you are, in effect, contributing a sense of scale as well as giving height in what might otherwise prove to be a flat site and one lacking in interest. In deciding which are for you, consider not only the ultimate height and spread, but shape and form, color and texture of bark, flowering period, possible fruits and berries, as well as interest of leaf and potential show in the fall.

Acer platanoides **'Drummondii'** A Norway maple noted for its variegated leaf. 20 × 15ft/6 × 4.5m

Cornus controversa **'Variegata'** Very, very slow but almost without equal. 15 × 15ft/4.5 × 4.5m

Halesia monticola Flowering in late spring, the snowdrop tree requires lime-free soil. 13 × 10ft/4 × 3m

Pyrus salicifolia **'Pendula'** An ornamental pear with small white flowers in spring. 20 × 15ft/6 × 4.5m

Robinia pseudoacacia **'Frisia'** This form of false acacia is noted for its golden yellow foliage. 26 × 20ft/8 × 6m

Caragana arborescens **'Lorbergii'** Known as the pea tree on account of late spring, pea-like flowers. 13 × 13ft/4 × 4m

Magnolia × loebneri **'Leonard Messel'**
Spring-flowering magnolias are a lovely
choice for the small garden, particularly
where the soil is lime free. 26 × 20ft/8 × 6m

Laburnum watereri **'Vossii'** Well loved for
the long yellow tassels in early summer.
15 × 10ft/4.5 × 3m

The intense blue of an early spring sky highlights the
purity of the starry flowered *Magnolia stellata*, which
can be grown as a small tree or a shrub (see page 138).

Malus × schiedeckeri **'Red Jade'** Many forms of malus are suited to the smaller garden and all blossom well in the spring. 13 × 20ft/4 × 6m

Prunus **'Amanogawa'** The attraction of this particular Japanese cherry is its column-like habit. Flowers in spring. 20 × 6ft/6 × 2m

Tamarix tetrandra This variety of tamarisk is smothered in pale pink plumes in summer. 13 × 13ft/4 × 4m

***Salix caprea* 'Kilmarnock'** The Kilmarnock willow is clothed with silvery catkins in the spring. 6 × 6ft/2 × 2m

Here in 'A Garden Writer's Garden' (see page 62) the Kilmarnock willow has been closely clipped.

***Salix alba* subsp. *vitellina* 'Britzensis'** Carried out in the early part of the year such severe pruning keeps this shrubby tree to a manageable size. 10 × 10ft/ 3 × 3m

Fully clothed by midsummer, this represents a single season's growth of 'Britzensis'.

Laurus nobilis Bay will lend itself readily to shaping when it will make an attractive specimen tree. E, 39 × 33ft/12 × 10m

Carpinus betulus Common hornbeam may be kept to a moderate size by clipping to shape. 39 × 26ft/12 × 8m

Euonymus fortunei Evergreen euonymus has been trimmed to become a standard tree. 16 × 16ft/5 × 5m

127

Acer palmatum* var. *dissectum As the year advances foliage of this maple turns to bright red. 5 × 8ft/1.5 × 2.4m

Amelanchier lamarckii Young copper-colored foliage sets off white flowers in spring. 15 × 15ft/4.5 × 4.5m

Acer palmatum atropurpureum Bronze leaves redden as the fall approaches. 15 × 15ft/4.5 × 4.5m

Rhus typhina Glorious fall color is the outstanding feature of the Stag's Horn Sumach. 10 × 10ft/3 × 3m

Sorbus vilmorinii The attraction of this graceful tree is twofold: flame foliage in the fall and decorative pink fruits. 16 × 16ft/5 × 5m

Clerodendrum trichotomum An outstanding small tree with starry white flowers in late summer. 13 × 13ft/4 × 4m

Acer griseum The paper-bark maple is most aptly named. 26 × 20ft/8 × 6m

Small, slow growing conifers add year-round interest and are low on maintenance.

An Irish yew, *Taxus baccata* 'Fastigiata', plays host to a climbing rose. The yew, ultimately, will reach a height of some 15ft/4.5m.

Abies balsamea f. *hudsonia* This very small conifer is appropriate for a rock garden. E, 3 × 3ft/1 × 1m

Chamaecyparis lawsoniana **'Minima Aurea'** Within this scree bed this dwarf conifer gives height. E, 4 × 4ft/ 1.2 × 1.2m

***Juniperus communis* 'Compressa'** For something really tiny, then choose this column-like form of juniper.
E, 30 × 6in/75 × 15cm

***Juniperus sabina* 'Tamariscifolia'** The spreading habit of the Savin juniper makes it ideal as ground cover.
E, 3 × 6ft/1 × 2m

***Picea* var. *albertiana* 'Conica'** Bright, fresh foliage tips are a mark of this small spruce. E, 6 × 3ft/2 × 1m

***Thuja orientalis* 'Aurea Nana'** Perfectly at home in the alpine garden.
E, 3ft × 30in/1m × 75cm

Shrubs – Border Structure

Borders which are entirely made up of annuals and perennials have a tendency to look flat and uninteresting once the main flowering season is past. This is particularly so in late fall or early spring when old stems have been cut back to ground level and the earth is bare.

By planting mixed borders, where shrubs and herbaceous plants are combined, it is possible to achieve a much more balanced, structured look. Fortunately there are many highly attractive shrubs which, on account of their slow growth or restricted size, are very well suited to the small garden. Choose them for interesting leaf, sometimes variegated, sometimes evergreen, for flower, for scent, for fruit and for a spectacular fall show. Larger shrubs, which may be too desirable to omit altogether from the garden, will usually respond well to judicious pruning, which carried out periodically, will keep them well within bounds.

Of course shrubs do not have to be grown in a border. Many are eminently suited to pot cultivation and will thrive under such conditions providing that they are not allowed to dry out, are fed regularly and do not become pot bound.

Chaenomeles **'Pink Lady'** Crimson flowers in spring. 10 × 10ft/3 × 3m

Ribes speciosum Arching stems carry deep red, fuchsia-like flowers in late spring and early summer. 6 × 6ft/ 2 × 2m

***Pieris forrestii* 'Forest Flame'** Bright scarlet shoots typify new growth on this slow-growing, evergreen shrub. ◐, E, 6 × 13ft/2 × 4m

Forsythia* × *intermedia This easy to grow spring shrub continues to retain its popularity, not least on account of its early sparkling color. 10 × 6ft/ 3 × 2m

Berberis darwinii Golden flowers of spring are followed in the fall with purple berries. E, 13 × 13ft/4 × 4m

***Helianthemum* 'Golden Queen'** All the rock roses flower over a considerable period. E, 1 × 3ft/ 30cm × 1m

Lupinus arboreus The tree lupin is in flower throughout the early summer. Semi-E, 5 × 5ft/1.5 × 1.5m

Philadelphus coronarius **'Aureus'** Grown especially for its warm yellow foliage, this form of mock orange is well suited to the smaller garden. Avoid planting in full sunlight which can, on occasion, cause scorching of new growth. 6 × 6ft/ 2 × 2m

Azara lanceolata Very pretty, rather wispy flowers in spring are set off by long, tapering shiny green leaves. E, 6 × 6ft/2 × 2m

Fothergilla major Sweetly scented flowers in the early part of the year to be followed by vivid fall color. 10 × 10ft/3 × 3m

Potentilla fruticosa Dwarf shrub in flower throughout the summer. 4 × 4ft/ 1.2 × 1.2m

Daphne × burkwoodii Enjoy deliciously scented daphnes in the first part of the year when their fragrance can fill the entire garden. 4 × 4ft/1.2 × 1.2m

Buddleja crispa Not totally hardy, it must be given a warm, protected situation. Flowers late summer. ◯, 8 × 8ft/ 2.4 × 2.4m

Syringa × persica A compact form of lilac. Prune lightly when the first flowers of spring are spent. 6 × 6ft/2 × 2m

***Weigela florida* 'Variegata'** The mass of pink bloom appears in the early spring. All weigelas enjoy a sunny, open position in the garden. ○, 5 × 5ft/1.5 × 1.5m

Lonicera tatarica Flowers cluster during late spring on this shrubby honeysuckle. 4 × 4ft/1.2 × 1.2m

***Prunus tenella* 'Firehill'** An ideal shrub in a spring border for its candyfloss flowers. ○, 6 × 6ft/2 × 2m

137

Chaenomeles speciosa **'Nivalis'** This quince will produce creamy-white flowers continuously in springtime. 8 × 16ft/ 2.4 × 5m

Viburnum plicatum A splendid shrub decked with blooms in the late spring. 10 × 13ft/3 × 4m

Magnolia stellata Star-shaped flowers appear on the bare stems in the early spring. Very slow-growing. 10 × 13ft/ 3 × 4m

Exochorda × *macrantha* **'The Bride'** Wreathed in flower for the spring it is ideally suited as a host plant for a late climber. ○, 8 × 10ft/2.4 × 3m

Viburnum × *juddii* Deeply fragrant spring flowers. This viburnum succeeds best in soil which is free-draining. 5 × 5 ft/ 1.5 × 1.5m

Spiraea nipponica **'Snowmound'** Early summer sees this easy-to-grow shrub heavily laden with pure white flowers. 8 × 8ft/2.4 × 2.4m

Choisya **'Aztec Pearl'** Another form of Mexican orange blossom which is a change from *C. ternata*. E, 6 × 6ft/2 × 2m

Rhododendron **Hybrid 'Bric-à-Brac'** Flowers bloom as early as the late winter but may be vulnerable to sharp frosts. E, 5 × 5ft/1.5 × 1.5m

Roses — Queen of Shrubs

Fortunately there is no reason at all why any garden, however small, should be denied at least one of these choicest of shrubs. From old-fashioned types to those small enough for the tiniest patio, there is something for every situation.

'Iceberg' No-one can but admire the habit of this prolific Floribunda. Ideal for a mixed border where it will flower for many months. 4 × 4ft/1.2 × 1.2m

'Yvonne Rabier' A dwarf polyantha rose. 4 × 3ft/1.2 × 1m

'Little White Pet' Small enough to grow in a pot. 2 × 2ft/60 × 60cm

'Gentle Touch' This truly is a miniature rose. 1½ft/45cm

Growing roses as standards is one way of overcoming a lack of space. In this situation the velvety blooms of the classically shaped 'Royal William' rise over a base of *Hedera canariensis*. The fast-growing, half hardy ivy acts as an ideal foil to the deeply crimson rose flowers.

'Jacques Cartier'
Compact, repeat flowering
Damask rose. 4 × 3ft/
1.2 × 1m

'The Fairy' Lovely sprays
of delicate pale-pink
rosettes. 2 × 3ft/
60cm × 1m

'Cécile Brunner' Sweetly
scented blooms are shaped
like a miniature Hybrid
Tea. 3 × 2ft/1m × 60cm

'Heritage' One of many recent introductions which as a group have become known
as English Roses. They combine repeat flowering with a sturdy, compact habit.
4 × 4ft/1.2 × 1.2m

'Amber Queen' A spreading Floribunda with a sweet scent. 2 × 2ft/ 60 × 60cm

'The Pilgrim' Rosettes of soft yellow on this freely flowering English Rose. 3½ × 3ft/1.1 × 1m

'Symphony' Similar in size and habit to 'The Pilgrim', this rose carries numerous scented blooms. 3 × 3ft/1 × 1m

'Mountbatten' A useful border rose with its dark foliage and luminous double flowers. 4 × 3ft/1.2 × 1m

A FURTHER SELECTION
OF ROSES

'Agnes'
'Alfred de Dalmas'
'De Meaux'
'Fimbriata'
'Hermosa'
'La Ville de Bruxelles'
'Léda'
'Mundi'
'Nathalie Nypels'
'Old Blush China'
R. pimpinellifolia
'Pink Bells'
'Pretty Polly'
'Simba'
'Souvenir de la Malmaison'
'Stanwell Perpetual'

Climbers – Front Line Candidates

That climbers climb, and in so doing occupy very little space at ground level, makes them invaluable plants for the small garden where space is, inevitably, restricted. Not only that, but they provide an almost limitless range of form, habit, flower color, leaf texture and shape, as well as suggesting something of interest for even the least promising and most difficult of situations.

Use climbers, particularly those which are evergreen, to help block out unsightly surroundings, to screen utilities, to mask unattractive walls and fences or to draw the eye away from a less than appealing viewpoint. Trained to scramble through host plants, such as trees and shrubs, climbers may be used to introduce a secondary canopy of color and interest.

Clematis macropetala **'Markham's Pink'**
Sugar-pink flowers smother this clematis
in the early spring. 6ft/1.8m

Clematis alpina **'Frances Rivis'** (shown
opposite) is also early into flower.
6ft/1.8m

Clematis alpina **'Ruby'** Plant this charming spring-flowering clematis in a sunny spot to capture the intensity of the dusky mauve-red flowers. 6ft/1.8m

Clematis alpina **'Willy'** All of these spring clematis of moderate growth would be suitable for a pot or container. 6ft/1.8m

Clematis macropetala **'Maidwell Hall'** All of the macropetala clematis put on one of the best displays of spring. 6ft/1.8m

Clematis montana **'Elizabeth'** Lovely in flower in spring but not entirely suitable for the small garden. 20ft/6m

Clematis chrysocoma Not dissimilar to the montanas but considerably less vigorous. 20ft/6m

Clematis **'Nelly Moser'** Position in partial shade to prevent the rosy-mauve sepals from fading in strong sunlight. Spring flowers are repeated in late summer. 10ft/3m

Clematis '**Lady Northcliffe**' Seldom without flower from mid to late summer. 6ft/1.8m

Clematis '**Étoile de Malicorne**' This clematis is used here to clothe the lower reaches of a yew hedge. Flowers early summer. 6ft/1.8m

Clematis '**Mrs. Cholmondeley**' Vigorous growth of this lovely hybrid may be restricted by hard pruning in the early part of the year. Flowers from early summer. 20ft/6m

Clematis **'Kathleen Wheeler'** The white rose is a perfect backdrop to the flowers of this bushy climber. 8ft/2.4m

Clematis **'Elsa Späth'** A mass of midsummer flowers is followed by a second flush later. 6ft/1.8m

Clematis **'Barbara Dibley'** The moderate growth of this gorgeous purple-red hybrid makes it most appropriate for any number of situations. Flowers early summer. 6ft/1.8m

Clematis **'Niobe'** To achieve the maximum number of flowers, prune 'Niobe' only lightly at the start of the year. A hard prune will delay the flowering period until late summer. 8ft/2.4m

Pictured right are three highly desirable clematis to provide color from midsummer onwards.

First to flower is *C.* × *jackmanii*, well known to gardeners and non-gardeners alike. A strong color, good performance and reliability combine to make it a popular choice.

Late-flowering viticella hybrids are amongst the most appealing of all clematis. Shown here are 'Madame Julia Correvon', in shades of deep red, and 'Purpurea Plena Elegans' whose double rosy-purple flowers are an absolute delight.

Wisteria floribunda This has been very
successfully grown up a stout pole.
Flowers early summer. ○, 30ft/9m

***Wisteria floribunda* 'Alba'** Racemes of
pure white flowers in early summer.
Prune in winter and summer. ○, 30ft/9m

Lonicera etrusca Unfortunately this
beautiful creamy-yellow honeysuckle is
not reliably hardy. Flowers summer/
fall. ○, 13ft/4m

***Lonicera japonica* 'Halliana'** A rapidly
growing evergreen. Flowers, which appear
in summer, are perfumed. E, 13ft/4m

Hydrangea anomala petiolaris Slow to establish, the self-clinging, climbing hydrangea is a splendid climber, producing these large, creamy-white flowers in summer even in a shady position. 26ft/8m

Actinidia kolomikta Such unusual leaf markings distinguish this climber of moderate growth. Plant in full sun to achieve best variegation. 12ft/3.5m

Climbing Roses

Roses epitomize early summer with their heavenly fragrance and lovely, lovely blooms in a range of delicious colors. In the small garden it may not always be possible to cultivate some of the old-fashioned shrub roses on account of the space they demand if they are to be grown well. An easy solution is to include in the garden a number of climbing roses.

Make your choice with care. Rambler roses are likely to prove far too vigorous and even some of the climbers may, when established, be in danger of outgrowing their allotted space. Select, where possible, those with a recurrent flowering pattern for they will provide interest over a much longer period.

Rosa **'Blush Noisette'** These pretty flowers, sweetly scented, will be continuous all summer long. 7ft/2.2m

Rosa **'Golden Showers'** This climber will provide a succession of blooms even against a sunless wall. 10ft/3m

***Rosa* 'Climbing Iceberg'** The climbing form produces flowers unstintingly over a long period. 10ft/3m

***Rosa* 'Variegata di Bologna'** This rose is only slightly recurrent but its unusual colorings make up for that. 10ft/3m

***Rosa* 'Buff Beauty'** This wonderfully scented rose may easily be trained as a climber. 10ft/3m

Wall Shrubs

In a small garden, where every plant must more than earn its keep, learn to experiment. Always remember that in an enclosed space you are possibly creating a warm micro-climate where many plants, previously thought of as unsuitable for the garden, will not only survive but thrive.

Close planting will also afford protection from the worst of the weather and you may always, in periods of intense cold, place bracken, sacking or any other porous material around the base of the shrub.

Abutilon megapotamicum Placed against a sunny wall this shrub will reward with these brightly colored, red and yellow flowers towards summer's end. E, 8ft/2.4m

Carpenteria californica Evergreen foliage of a glossy, bright green forms a background to these stunning, fragrant flowers which bloom throughout the mid-summer. 5 × 5ft/1.5 × 1.5m

Rhodochiton atrosanguineus This exotic climber may, in cold areas, be grown as an annual. ○, 10ft/3m

Robinia kelseyi Its flowers in late spring are an extremely impressive sight. ○, 8ft/2.4m

157

Passiflora caerulea Blooms in summer and fall are followed by small fruits. ○, 20ft/6m

Lavatera maritima bicolor A free-flowering tree mallow which should be pruned hard in the early spring. 5ft/1.5m

Eccremocarpus scaber Orange and red tubular flowers in summer. ○, 13ft/4m

***Ceanothus* 'Blue Mound'** A glorious, blue-flowered shrub for the early summer which, lovely as it is, would make a superb host for climbers. ○, E, 5 × 6ft/1.5 × 2m

Abutilon × suntense
Flowers in late spring and
early summer. ○, 8ft/2.4m

× *Fatshedera lizei* These
grand leaves would make a
splendid backdrop. E,
6 × 10ft/2 × 3m

***Solanum crispum* 'Glasnevin'** Smothered in flower for
most of the summer. Frost hardy to 23°F/−5°C. ○, E or
semi-E, 20ft/6m

Callistemon pallidus
Flowers of the 'bottle
brush' in early summer are
a delight. Soil should be
acidic, well drained and the
plant placed in full sun. E,
10ft/3m

Perennials — Flowers For Every Season

Gardening on whatever scale, perennials are as invaluable as they are essential. Not only do they cover an enormous range of flowering plants, but they also include fashionable grasses, sedges and ferns. Some, on account of their height and spread, a tendency to be invasive or to seed around too freely, must be omitted. Others with a very short flowering season, or a reluctance to flower, however desirable, should be passed over in favor of those which represent much better value. And for this there is no shortage of choice.

However, do not allow yourself to be too cautious. A garden filled with perennial plants of uniform height and even spread will be totally lacking in interest. Some plants may be included simply on account of their size where their greatest impact will be made in a restricted space. Likewise tall-growing plants placed at the front of the border will introduce variety of pattern.

Epimedium × youngianum **'Roseum'**
Rose-colored flowers rise from a base of leaves in the early spring. 10in × 1ft/25 × 30cm

Primula vulgaris A cool, slightly shady spot is ideal for early-flowering primrose. 4in/10cm

Convallaria majalis Unfussy about where it is grown. Flowers open in spring. ◑, ●, 8in/20cm

***Lamium maculatum* 'White Nancy'** Lighten a dull corner with this free-flowering form of dead-nettle. 6in × 2ft/15 × 60cm

***Dicentra* 'Bacchanal'** Deepest red flowers are borne in profusion throughout the spring. 1in × 1ft/30 × 30cm

Primula denticulata* var. *alba White rounded heads at the beginning of the year. ◑, 8in × 1ft/20 × 30cm

Uvularia grandiflora Grow the bellwort for its graceful and certainly different spring flowers. Ideally it prefers a moist, slightly acid soil in some shade. ◐, 1 × 1ft/ 30 × 30cm

***Ajuga reptans* 'Catlin's Giant'** In spring large blue flower heads appear on this particularly good form of bugle. E, 6in × 2ft/15 × 60cm

Galium ordoratum The white star flowers appear in spring and are long-lasting. 8in × 1ft/20 × 30cm

Iris graminea Shaded purple flowers in late spring nestle amongst lustrous foliage in the plum tart iris. ◑, 1 × 1ft/ 30 × 30cm

***Sedum* 'Ruby Glow'** For end-of-year color when the crimson flowers come into their own. ○, 1 × 1ft/30 × 30cm

***Campanula punctata* 'Rubriflora'** Light maroon tubular bells provide summer color over many weeks. 1 × 1ft/30 × 30cm

163

***Phlox carolina* 'Bill Baker'** Constant dead-heading will reward with flowers from early summer through very many weeks. 1 × 1ft/30 × 30cm

***Phlox divaricata* 'May Breeze'** An early-flowering phlox in cool white with a subtle hint of lilac. 1ft × 8in/30 × 20cm

Dianthus gratianopolitanus All of the old-fashioned pinks like to be baked in full sun. Summer-flowering. ○, E, 8in × 1½ft/20 × 45cm

Geranium renardii An attractive, purple-veined flower in early summer is complemented by soft grey-green foliage. ◐, 1 × 1ft/30 × 30cm

Geranium endressii Pretty pink flowers are carried over several weeks in summer. 2 × 2ft/60 × 60cm

***Geranium pratense* 'Mrs. Kendall Clark'** In summer the appeal of this particular cranesbill is the flower color. 2¹⁄₂ × 1¹⁄₂ft/75 × 45cm

***Geranium cinereum* 'Ballerina'** Flowers are carried over a long period in summer. 8in × 1ft/20 × 30cm

Helleborus orientalis Early-flowering hellebores are amongst the most desirable of all spring flowers. ◑, 1¹/₂ × 1¹/₂ft/ 45 × 45cm

Eryngium variifolium Sea-hollies add texture to the border in late summer. ○, 1¹/₂ft × 10in/45 × 25cm

Persicaria campanulata This hardy perennial will provide color until the first frosts of the fall. 3 × 3ft/1 × 1m

Euphorbia nicaeensis An absolutely spectacular plant on account of its foliage. ○, E, 1¹/₂ × 2ft/40 × 60cm

Using plants together effectively is so very important in a small garden. Here grey-leafed hostas are captured at flowering time alongside the feathery plumes of white and coral astilbes.

***Nepeta* 'Six Hills Giant'** Once the main summer flowering period is over, cut back a second flush. ○, 2 × 2ft/60 × 60cm

***Polemonium reptans* 'Lambrook Mauve'** This Jacob's Ladder delights with flowers in summer. 2 × 2ft/60 × 60cm

Scabiosa caucasica Lovely violet-blue scabious for an eye-catching summer display. ◯, 2 × 2ft/60 × 60cm

Salvia sclarea* var. *turkestanica Self-seeded plantlets will appear in the spring and flower the following summer. 2¹/₂ × 1ft/75 × 30cm

Iris pallida* ssp. *pallida Bold plantings of irises for early summer give to any border a sense of purpose and of deliberate planning. The effect of one variety is so much better than that of mixed colors. ◯, 1¹/₂ × 1ft/45 × 30cm

Knautia macedonica Wine-red, scabious-like knautia in a summer display with lavender-blue veronica. 1¹/₂ × 1¹/₂ft/ 45 × 45cm

***Salvia* × *superba* 'Mainacht'** Stiff spikes of deep violet-blue flowers from mid to late summer. 1¹/₂ × 1¹/₂ft/45 × 45cm

***Aquilegia* hybrid** Long-spurred columbines should self-seed to give a well-furnished look in spring and summer. 3 × 1¹/₂ft/1m × 45cm

Thalictrum aquilegiifolium Use fluffy meadow rue to contribute an air of lightness in summer. $2^{1}/_{2} \times$ 2ft/75 $\times$ 60cm

***Paeonia lactiflora* 'Bowl of Beauty'** Peonies should be enjoyed in summer for their wonderful, if somewhat blowzy, flowers. 3 $\times$ 3ft/1 $\times$ 1m

Papaver orientale Flowering in early summer, their dying foliage needs to be disguised. 3 $\times$ 2ft/1m $\times$ 60cm

Diascia vigilis All of the diascias contribute vibrant color over a very long period in smmer. $1^{1}/_{2} \times 1^{1}/_{2}$ft/45 $\times$ 45cm

Alstroemeria **'Ligtu Hybrids'** There is something slightly exotic about the summer blooms of the alstroemeria. ○, 2 × 1ft/60 × 30cm

Lychnis chalcedonica Long-lasting, scarlet flower heads add vibrant color to the early summer border. 3 × 1½ft/ 1m × 45cm

Penstemon **'Apple Blossom'** Penstemons make excellent border plants not least because of their long flowering period in summer. ○, 2 × 1½ft/60 × 45cm

Crocosmia **'Vulcan'** Crocosmias are useful plants in the border from mid-summer onwards. 3 × 1ft/1m × 30cm

Smilacina racemosa will produce these flowery plumes in quite shady conditions in late spring. $2\frac{1}{2} \times 2\frac{1}{2}$ft/75 × 75cm

Polygonatum × hybridum Solomon's seal has arching stems and late spring bell-shaped flowers. $3 \times 1\frac{1}{2}$ft/1m × 45cm

Sisyrinchium striatum In summer from iris-like foliage arise rather strange little creamy flowers. 2×1ft/60 × 30cm

Lysimachia clethroides Charming with other whites, or partnered with blue or the palest of lemon. Flowers in late summer. 3×1ft/1m × 30cm

Dictamnus albus purpureus A gentle, misty, early summer combination of the pale purple dictamnus set against the snow-white blooms of *Rosa* 'Iceberg'. 2 × 2ft/60 × 60cm

Gillenia trifoliata Use it in summer as a graceful filler between other showier plants. 3 × 2ft/1m × 60cm

Stachys macrantha Distinctive, purplish summer flowers are highlighted here with annual white nigella. 1½ × 1½ft/ 45 × 45cm

Kniphofia **'Little Maid'** Creamy-yellow spikes, touched with green, are subdued enough for a quiet summer scheme. 2 × 1½ft/60 × 45cm

Asphodeline lutea Yellow, star-like summer flowers hugging a tall-growing, thin-leafed stem. 3 × 2ft/1m × 60cm

Veronica gentianoides **'Tissington White'** Edge a border with a row of this pale blue-white veronica. Ground-hugging leaves remain evergreen, the flowers appearing from mid-spring. ○, 10 × 8in/25 × 20cm

***Anthemis tinctoria* 'Alba'** Dead-head this perenial to enjoy a succession in mid-summer of these creamy flowers.
○, 2¹/₂ × 2¹/₂ft/75 × 75cm

Inula barbata These bright yellow daisy flowers may be enjoyed well into the fall.
○, 2 × 1¹/₂ft/60 × 45cm

***Rudbeckia fulgida* 'Goldsturm'** This prolific late summer perennial may be relied upon to flower for several months. In this border it is partnered with *Helenium* 'Golden Youth' of similar color. ○, 2¹/₂ × 1¹/₂ft/75 × 45cm

***Aster × frikartii* 'Mönch'** One of the best Michaelmas daisies because of its long-flowering period from mid-simmer. Here it forms a background to the perennial *Agastache* 'Blue Fortune'. ◯, 2¹/₂ × 1¹/₂ft/75 × 45cm

***Hemerocallis* 'Summer Wine'** Swept-back flower heads from mid to late summer possess a velvety quality. 3 × 3ft/1 × 1m

***Phlox* 'Norah Leigh'** The attraction of this summer-flowering phlox is not simply its flower but rather its leaves. ◯, 2¹/₂ × 2ft/75 × 60cm

As the fall approaches the cone flowers come into their own. Pictured here are *Echinacea purpurea* and *E. purpurea* 'White Swan'. $2^{1}/_{2} \times 1^{1}/_{2}$ft/ 75×45cm

Campanula lactiflora Drift this campanula through the back of the summer border. 4 × 2ft/1.2m × 60cm

Campanula latifolia alba Plant in slight shade for the greatest intensity of color. Summer-flowering. 4 × 1ft/1.2m × 30cm

***Aconitum carmichaelii* 'Barker's Variety'** Late-flowering monkshood is a poisonous plant which somehow in appearance is slightly sinister. 5 × 1ft/1.5m × 30cm

***Phlox paniculata* 'Fujiyama'** Large flower heads in late summer of pure white are scented. ○, 3 × 2¹/₂ft/ 1m × 75cm

Crambe cordifolia Such a plant as this, with its wonderful, frothy summer flowers, themselves scented, is, at a glance, irresistible. ○, 6 × 4ft/2 × 1.2m

Alcea rugosa Tall-growing, perennial hollyhocks give height and stature to a garden in summer and early fall. 6 × 1¹/₂ft/2m × 45cm

Cephalaria gigantea Thin stems enable it to be positioned quite close to the front of the summer border. 6 × 1¹/₂ft/ 2m × 45cm

Verbascum chaixii 'Album' Stately verbascums simply have to be included in the garden. Summer-flowering. 5 × 1¹/₂ft/1.5m × 45cm

Lobelia syphilitica Unfortunately this lobelia is not hardy in any but the most sheltered of gardens. Flowers late summer to fall. 4 × 1ft/1.2m × 30cm

Delphinium In some ways no garden should be without such a traditional and much loved summer flower as the delphinium. Select from a wide range of large flowered hybrids. ○, 8 × 3ft/2.4 × 1m but depends on type.

***Aster novi-belgii* 'Goliath'** Free-flowering asters contribute color to late summer borders and well into the fall. ○, 4 × 1¹⁄₂ft/1.2m × 45cm

Anemone* × *hybrida Japanese anemones are one of the principal delights of the end-of-year garden. 5 × 1¹⁄₂ft/ 1.5m × 45cm

Annuals, Biennials, Half-Hardy Perennials – for Fast Effects

For continuous color through much of the growing season, then there is little to rival a show of annuals. Usually raised from seed, these plants will reach flowering point within a very short space of time.

And there is something to satisfy every possible taste, every conceivable garden situation. For sheer brilliance there are the bedding salvias, *Salvia splendens*, French and African marigolds, colorful petunias, blue and purple lobelias and cheerful impatiens. For scent, include old-fashioned stocks, surfinia, nemesia and, of course, fragrant nicotiana, the tobacco plant, with its powerful, heady perfume. To create an exotic look, suggestive of hot, sunny climates, there are lotus plants, half-hardy osteospermums, tender argyranthemums and fabulous gazanias. For those looking for the understated, ethereal look, then try early white nigella to be followed with late flowering, white cosmos.

Helianthus Sunflowers are such fun. Allow them to soar up at the back of the border! ○, 7ft/2.2m or more

Helichrysum These colorful strawflowers may also be very effectively dried for indoor flower arrangements. ○, 2 × 1ft/60 × 30cm

Clarkia elegans Clarkia will create an harmonious display in the early summer. ○, 2 × 1ft/60 × 30cm

Digitalis purpurea Traditional, biennial foxgloves remain a firm favourite for mid-summer. ◑, 4 × 1ft/1.2m × 30cm

Argyranthemum **'Vancouver'** Tender Paris daisies or marguerites are an excellent choice for pots. ○, 3 × 3ft/ 1 × 1m

Cosmos Annual cosmos may be relied upon for its length of flowering. 3 × 2ft/1m × 60cm

***Arctotis* × *hybrida* 'Wine'** Treat as an annual in colder areas. Flowers from summer into the fall. ◐, 1½ × 1ft/ 45 × 30cm

Felicia amelloides These clear blue, yellow-centered heads will sparkle with color all summer long. ◐, 1½ × 1ft/45 × 30cm

Lavatera trimestris A free-flowering, half-hardy annual closely related to the shrubby mallow. ◐, 2 × 1ft/60 × 30cm

Zonal Pelargonium Countless varieties ensure the popularity of what are widely known as summer geraniums. ◐, 1½ft/ 45cm

No garden can really be complete without a share,
however small, of the quintessential sweet William, or
Dianthus barbatus. A reliable biennial, they may,
once established, be left to themselves
to set seed and come again.
Lovely in the summer
border, they also make
excellent flowers
to cut and
arrange in
water
indoors.

Nicotiana Tobacco plants of pale salmon–pink are teamed here with toning impatiens. ○, 1–3 × 1–1¹/₂ft/ 30–90 × 30–45cm

Zinnia Sown in situ in late spring, zinnias provide a wealth of easy summer color. ○, 2¹/₂ × 1ft/75 × 30cm

Nigella damascena With such an evocative name as 'love-in-a-mist', it is difficult to resist these annuals. 1¹/₂ft × 8in/ 45 × 20cm

Heliotrope Deep blue or violet flowers are strongly scented of cherry pie. ○, 1¹/₂ × 1ft/45 × 30cm

Antirrhinum Snapdragons conjure up memories of childhood. These, of intense orange-red, are a small sample of all the bright colors which may be grown. ○, 1ft × 6in/30 × 15cm

Tagetes patula French marigolds produce flowers continuously throughout the summer. ○, 10in/25cm

Tagetes This particular variety of French marigold boasts double flowers. ○, 10in/25cm

Universal Pansies Wonderful, cheery faces in all manner of color combinations make these winter pansies such a popular choice. Even severe frosts will not entirely put a stop to their flowering. 6in/15cm

Limnanthes douglasii Frequently referred to as poached egg plants, ideal as an edging from early summer. ◯, 6in/15cm

Calendula officinalis All of the true marigolds are noted for simplicity and ease, flowering from spring to fall. ◯, 1¹/₂ × 1ft/45 × 30cm

Gazania 'Dorothy' Available in a whole range of colors. Position in a sunny place for the flowers to open. ○, 1ft × 8in/ 30 × 20cm

Chrysanthemum parthenium Noted for distinctly aromatic leaves and flowers of a long-lasting quality. ○, 9 × 6in/ 23 × 15cm

Viola **'Sorbet Mixed'** So many very different strains of pansy from which to choose, none of which ever looks out of place. 4in × 1ft/10 × 30cm

Godetia Chalice-shaped flowers make splendid border plants. 8–12in/20–30cm

***Schizanthus* × *wintonensis* 'Hit Parade'** The poor man's orchid is among the most beautiful of all annuals. ◯, 1ft/30cm

Salvia splendens Scarlet blooms never fail to make an impact. ◯, 1ft/30cm

Nemesia Nemesia will trail a blaze of color through the border.
◯, 1–1¹/₂ft/30–45cm

***Salpiglossis* 'Casino'** Trumpet-shaped flowers in vibrant color mixes make these showy annuals strong candidates for any scheme. ◑, 2–3ft/60–90cm

A border like this one, closely packed with summer-flowering fuchsias, provides non-stop color for the greater part of the summer.

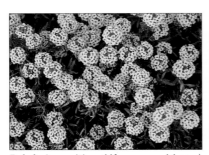

Lobularia maritima (Alyssum maritimum)
Often used as an edging plant. Available also in pink and lilac. ○, 3in/7.5cm

Osteospermum **'Whirligig'** Beautifully shaped, sophisticated flowers for an open, sunny position. ○, 1 × 1ft/30 × 30cm

Senecio maritima Silver-leafed cineraria is a deservedly popular annual grown for its ornamental, deeply-cut foliage. Here it is placed as a spot plant among highly charged, bedding begonias. ○, 1 × 1ft/30 × 30cm

Impatiens Vibrant impatiens may be relied upon for color all summer.
1ft × 6in/30 × 15cm

Ageratum Coming into flower early on, ageratum will continue in bloom until fall. ○, 6in/15cm

Alpines and Rock Plants – Tiny Treasures

Of course alpines and rock plants lend themselves to the small garden. These are tiny little bulbs, perennials, shrubs, and even trees, which on account of their size sit comfortably and are at home in a small-scale landscape. They belong at the front of the border, in specially prepared rock gardens, on scree beds and in troughs, old sinks, pots and any other suitable container.

In the main they share a dislike of winter wet and are happiest when planted in free draining soil. To achieve this, heavy clay, or similar, should be broken down with the addition of generous quantities of grit.

This well furnished rock garden succeeds on account of the fact that it has been created mindful of scale. Stone has been used boldly and in such a way as to suggest a stratum of natural outcrop.

***Aubrieta* 'Barker's Double'** Aubrieta here is positioned in such a way as to spill over the rock face to provide a dramatic contrast with the grey stone, flowering from spring into early summer. ○, 2in × 1¹/₂ft/5 × 45cm

Iberis priutii Startlingly white flowers in late spring to early summer over dark, evergreen foliage, the whole appearing to come from some tiny crevice in the wall. ○, 6in × 1¹/₂ft/ 15 × 45cm

Sanguinaria canadensis
'Plena' Snowy-white
flowers appear in the early
part of spring. ◑, 4in/10cm

Ipheion uniflorum
'Violaceum' A bulb with
starry spring flowers.
6in/15cm

Iris pumila This miniature
iris has spread through the
gravel. Flowers mid-spring.
4in/10cm

***Lithodora diffusa* 'Star'** In early summer deep blue and white flowers marked, as its
name implies, with a star formation. 6in/15cm

Tulipa batalinii Above
wavy leaves rise soft, pale
yellow flowers in spring.
4in/10cm

Corydalis flexuosa This
striking blue flower appears
late spring. 1 × 1ft/
30 × 30cm

Dicentra cucullaria A
dainty white form of
bleeding heart. Spring-
flowering. 6in/15cm

Penstemon menziesii The flowers of this penstemon, which is one of many suitable for
the rock garden, open in early summer. 6in × 1ft/15 × 30cm

Double primulas, like this one, have become very collectable. Periodically, following flowering in spring, they should be divided. 4in/10cm

Eastertime is synonymous with the flowering of the pasque flower, *Pulsatilla vulgaris*.

Flowering at the same time is the showy little celandine in one of its cultivated forms. *Ranunculus* 'Brazen Hussey' well lives up to its name with its bold and brassy yellow flowers and deep bronze foliage.

Everyone is familiar with the primrose. Less commonly known is *Primula* 'Hose-in-Hose' where the usual primrose flower is surrounded by a ruff of miniature leaves.

Phlox bifida Another rockery phlox seen growing against and toning with a slate division. ○, E, 4in × 1ft/10 × 30cm

Mossy saxifrage These pretty flowers appear in the spring. Take the trouble to dead head. E, 6in × 1ft/15 × 30cm

***Phlox subulata* 'Betty'** Low-growing phlox flower in the late spring and early summer. ○, E, 4in × 1ft/10 × 30cm

Daphne cneorum On a still evening the perfume of this lovely, prostrate daphne will fill the entire garden. Rich pink flowers are carried above tiny evergreen leaves in spring. E, 1¹/₂ × 3ft/45 × 90cm

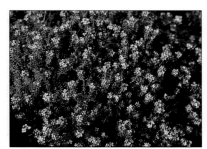

Aethionema 'Warley Rose' This shrub, smothered in flowers during the early summer, is semi-evergreen.
○, 6 × 9in/15 × 23cm

Androsace lanuginosa A mat–forming perennial which will bloom for much of the summer. 2in × 1ft/5 × 30cm

Arenaria montana Once the summer flowers are over, cut back hard. 6in × 1ft/15 × 30cm

Brunnera macrophylla (Siberian bugloss) Charming spring flowers. ◐, 1¹/₂ × 1¹/₂ft/45 × 45cm

Ajuga **'Pink Surprise'** An excellent carpet of foliage with flowers in spring. E, 6in × 2ft/15 × 60cm

Lamium roseum **'Wootton Pink'** (pictured left) An absolutely charming combination of clear pink flowers in late spring over gently variegated leaves. 6in × 1ft/15 × 30cm

Epimedium × youngianum **'Roseum'** Enjoy these interesting little flowers in the first part of the year. The leaves become quite bronze in the fall. 10in × 1ft/ 25 × 30cm

Alchemilla conjuncta Sprays of lime-green flowers from mid to late summer. 6in × 1ft/15 × 30cm

Alchemilla erythropoda A miniature lady's mantle which possesses all the good qualities of *A. mollis*. 6in × 1ft/15 × 30cm

Euphorbia myrsinites Place this spurge to drape over rocks or hang down the side of a low wall. Appearing in spring at the tips of fleshy, glaucous foliage are lime bracts. ○, E, 6in × 2ft/15 × 60cm

Gentiana sino-ornata Bright blue flowers for the fall. However, this gentian must be provided with moist, acid soil and sun. 3 × 9in/7.5 × 23cm

Campanula garganica forms tight rosettes of leaves against which are displayed blue starry flowers in summer. 6in × 1ft/ 15 × 30cm

Campanula '**Birch Hybrid**' is a quick growing, versatile plant to flower mid to late summer. 6in × 1ft/15 × 30cm

Omphalodes cappadocica '**Cherry Ingram**' A mass of blue flowers all the way through the spring. 6in × 1ft/ 15 × 30cm

Ramonda myconi Few alpines succeed in total shade. Ramonda is an exception. Flowers late spring/early summer. ●, E, 3 × 6in/7.5 × 15cm

Erinus alpinus Flowers in late spring and summer are combinations of red, mauve, pink or white. ○, E, 3 × 3in/7.5 × 7.5cm

Erigeron karvinskianus This self-seeder will place itself wherever it can gain a foothold. Flowers summer to fall. ○, 6in × 1ft/15 × 30cm

Armeria maritima It will produce in summer a succession of little rounded, pink flowers. ○, E, 4 × 8in/10 × 20cm

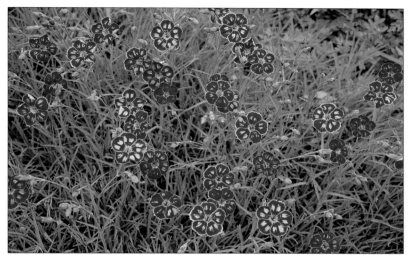

***Dianthus* 'Gravetye Gem'** Plant pinks not just on account of their scented flowers in summer but also for their rather spiky leaves. ○, E, 8in × 1ft/20 × 30cm

***Dianthus* 'Rose de Mai'** An abundance of summer flower. ○, E, 8in × 1¹/₂ft/ 20 × 45cm

Convolvulus sabatius Allow this convolvulus to trail its flowers in summer and early fall. ○, 6in × 1¹/₂ft/ 15 × 45cm

Bulbs — All Year Fillers

From the first snowdrops in late winter to nerines in the fall there are countless bulbs to give glamor and excitement to even the smallest of gardens.

The secret is to pack them in. Plant in generous groups to fill gaps between existing perennials, to complement and contrast with evergreens as well as to provide a changing focal pattern of pots on terrace or patio.

Generally bulbs enjoy good drainage. If your soil is heavy, or inclined to be water-logged, incorporate plenty of horticultural grit into the planting compost. In some instances it may be a good idea to rest the bulb itself on a layer of grit or gravel.

Cyclamen coum Even without their pretty late winter pink or white flowers, these cyclamen are highly desirable for their interestingly marbled leaves. ◑, 4in/10cm

Crocus tommasinianus Make a small space for these early spring flowers. 4in/10cm

Dutch crocus Crocus may be grown in the open ground, in either sun or shade, or massed in pots. 4in/10cm

Anemone blanda **'White Splendour'** These woodland anemones positively glow among the lower branches of a chaenomeles. 4in/10cm

Narcissus cyclamineus A long, protruding trumpet on this early spring daffodil. 6–8in/15–20cm

Narcissus bulbocodium Where space is at a premium miniature varieties, like this one, are ideal. ○, 6–8in/15–20cm

Narcissus 'February Gold' Of all the miniature daffodils this remains a firm favorite. 6–8in/15–20cm

Narcissus 'Hawera' thrives in a well-drained situation. 1¹/₂ft/45cm

Hyacinthoides italica Used as spring bedding here. 8in/20cm

Erythronium 'Citronella' Wonderful pale lemon spring flowers. The dog's tooth violet dies down in early summer. 6in/15cm

Tulipa 'Keizerskroon' This neglected corner has been brought to life with tulips and primrose 'White Shades'. 1¹/₂ft/45cm

Muscari plumosum These plume-like spring flowers are of a soft mauve. 10in/25cm

Tulipa **'Maréchal Niel'** The pale gold of the tulip has been artfully chosen to pick up and reflect the eye of the Universal pansy. 1¹/₂ft/45cm

***Anemone nemorosa* 'Robinsoniana'** It is difficult to resist this lovely, pale lavender form of the spring-flowering wood anemone. 6in/15cm

Tulipa **'Black Parrot'** These velvety parrot tulips form an integral part of a small yew enclosed garden. 1¹/₂ft/45cm

Fritillaria imperialis Crown imperials, in orange, red or yellow, are amongst the most striking of spring bulbs.
3 × 1ft/1m × 30cm

Fritillaria pyrenaica make an unusual addition to the spring garden. 1ft/30cm

Iris sibirica All the sibirica irises succeed best in moisture retentive soil. Flowers in early summer. ◯, 2 × 2ft/60 × 60cm

Allium aflatunense **'Purple Sensation'** These splendid ornamental onions should be placed to rise through other summer plantings. 3ft/1m

Nectaroscordum siculum Gracefully arching umbels. Grow in full sun or part shade through other foliage plants. 3ft/1m

Gladiolus byzantinus A small-flowered, early gladiolus which is sufficiently hardy to remain in the ground. 2ft/60cm

Eremurus bungei Foxtail lilies make a bold statement in mid-summer. ○, 5 × 2ft/1.5m × 60cm

Lilium martagon* var. *album Turk's cap lilies are easily grown in a semi-shaded position. 5 × 1ft/1.5m × 30cm

Allium moly An additional bonus to this brightly colored, summer-flowering yellow onion is that it is scented. 10in/25cm

Lilium regale The intoxicating fragrance of the regal lily is one of the delights of summer. They do particularly well when cultivated in pots. 4 × 1ft / 1.2m × 30cm

***Lilium* 'King Pete'** 'King Pete' is but one of many Asiatic hybrids from which to choose for summer flowers. 3 × 1ft / 1m × 30cm

Agapanthus **Headbourne Hybrids**
Grow agapanthus either in the open
ground or in pots for flowers in late
summer. ○, 2 × 1¹/₂ft/60 × 45cm

Eucomis bicolor The pineapple plant has
unusual green flowers in summer.
○, 1¹/₂ × 2ft/45 × 60cm

Fall crocus Even when planted in the
fall, these crocus will flower within three
to four weeks. 4in/10cm

Nerine bowdenii Gorgeously ostentatious
bulbs which come into their own as the
season draws to a close. ○, 1¹/₂ft × 8in/
45 × 20cm

Crinum powellii Plant in well drained soil for these flowers to give of their best in the fall. ◯, 3 × 2ft/1m × 60cm

***Dahlia* 'Gerrie Hoek'** All of the late-flowering dahlias bring much needed warmth to the fall borders. ◯, 2 × 2ft/60 × 60cm

Colchicum speciosum Colchicums require free draining soil in full sun. Fall-flowering. ◯, 8 × 8in/20 × 20cm

Cyclamen hederifolium Flowers, which appear before the foliage, bloom during the fall. 4 × 8in/10 × 20cm

Water Plants – A Profusion of Flowers and Foliage

Virtually any water feature, irrespective of how tiny it may be, will, almost certainly, appear somewhat naked without a clothing of associated leaf and flower. In addition to those plants which actually grow in water, marginal plantings will contribute to the overall appearance of the water garden in two distinct ways. First, they will help to suggest a natural look, giving to the immediate area the semblance of fertile, moisture-retentive ground, maybe even going so far as to hint at a miniature bog garden. Second, they will have a totally functional purpose, that of disguising the very mechanics by which any artificial water system is created.

Primula sieboldii Plant in damp soil in a position which is afforded some shelter. Flowers early summer. 8in × 1ft/20 × 30cm

Primula florindae This primula will bring color to the garden for many weeks in summer. ◑, 2¹/₂ × 2¹/₂ft/75 × 75cm

Primula pulverulenta This candelabra primula makes an exciting, eye-catching display during early summer. 3 × 1¹/₂ft/ 1m × 45cm

***Primula japonica* 'Postford White'** Flowering in early summer in a semi-shaded position. 1¹/₂ × 1¹/₂ft/45 × 45cm

Primula vialii Buds of bright scarlet slowly open to lavender in late spring. Position in rich, moist soil. 1 × 1ft/30 × 30cm

Astilbe × arendsii **'Erica'** All of the astilbes are noted for their feathery summer plumes and deeply cut foliage. 3 × 3ft/1 × 1m

Geum **'Red Wings'** A striking form of avens. Flowers appear in summer. ○, 1 × 1ft/30 × 30cm

Astilbe × arendsii **'Granat'** Deep, almost rust-red, flowers are a welcome change from pastel hues. 3 × 3ft/1 × 1m

Geum rivale **'Album'** A lovely, simple white form of avens. 2 × 2ft/60 × 60cm

Lobelia **'Dark Crusader'** Such a handsome, richly-colored perennial as this deserves to be given prominence in the garden. Flowers late summer. 3 × 1ft/1m × 30cm

Mimulus flower in summer but require soil conditions which remain damp throughout the year. 1 × 1ft/30 × 30cm

Camassia leichtlinii Violet–blue flowers rise in early summer in this moisture-loving perennial. 2¹/₂ × 1ft/75 × 30cm

Arisaema candidissimum Exotic plants which flower, before the leaves fully mature, in the early summer. 1 × 1ft/30 × 30cm

Dodecatheon meadia The shooting star is a beautiful plant for a damp spot. Spring-flowering. 1¹/₂ × 1ft/45 × 30cm

Schizostylis coccinea Kaffir lilies, blooming from late summer well into the fall, add a touch of brightness.
2 × 1ft/60 × 30cm

Chaerophyllum hirsutum '**Roseum**' Rather akin to cow parsley. The flowering period is during the late spring.
2 × 2ft/60 × 60cm

Filipendula rubra '**Venusta**' Tall-growing meadow-sweet carrying plentiful heads of the softest pink in mid-summer.
6 × 4ft/2 × 1.2m

Cardamine pratensis (**Lady's smock**) A perennial whose lilac flowers open in early spring. 10 × 4in/25 × 10cm

Caltha palustris Use as an edging to ponds or simply as a spring statement. ◯, 1 × 1¹/₂ft/30 × 45cm

Lysichiton americanus At the margins of the pond this will make a spectacular show in spring. 3 × 2¹/₂ft/1m × 75cm

Trollius europaeus Bright yellow heads of the globe flower are produced in spring. 2 × 2ft/60 × 60cm

***Iris* 'Holden Clough'** Beautiful markings in early summer on the falls of this iris. 2¹/₂ × 2¹/₂ft/75 × 75cm

Iris sibirica **'Soft Blue'** Clump-forming sibirica irises are most appealing border plants for early summer. 3 × 2ft/1m × 60cm

Trillium grandiflorum **'Roseum'** Rich soil, shade from the sun and immense patience are required for these spring flowers. ●, 15 × 12in/38 × 30cm

Iris missouriensis Obviously a small garden will not permit such a stand of irises in early summer. What is important, though, is to aim for bold effects. 2 × 2ft/60 × 60cm

***Houttuynia cordata* 'Chameleon'** This multi-colored, ground covering perennial will spread more than is always desirable. That said, it is not at all difficult to control. ◯, 4in/10cm

Matteuccia struthiopteris This ostrich fern is particularly attractive when the new fronds unfurl in springtime. 3 × 2ft/ 1m × 60cm

Rodgersia sambucifolia Large-leafed rodgersias do, naturally, take up space. However, they help to define a planting scheme. 3 × 3ft/1 × 1m

Hosta sieboldiana The glaucous leaves create interest from the point at which they open in the spring. ◐, 2¹/₂ × 2¹/₂ft/ 75 × 75cm

Onoclea sensibilis Use this prettily shaped fern as a dainty edging to a small pool. 1¹/₂ × 2ft/45 × 60cm

Use hostas, such as this splendid *H*. 'Halcyon' illustrated here, throughout the water garden to add form to other less definite plantings and, of course, to act as ground cover.

229

Aponogeton distachyos Include plants like the water hawthorn in a small pond to assist with oxygenation. Plant in up to 1½ft/45cm of water.

Myriophyllum aquaticum Parrot's feather thrives beneath the surface where it helps to keep the water clear.

Orontium aquaticum Another oxygenating plant but one with rather unusual, poker-like flowers of creamy-white tipped yellow in spring. Place this plant in up to 1ft / 30cm of water.

Nymphaea '**James Brydon**' Divide lilies every few years in the spring. Planting depth 9in–1¹/₂ft/23–45cm

Nymphaea '**Laydekeri Fulgens**' Usually lilies will flower from early summer until the first frosts. Planting depth 9in/23cm or more.

Nymphaea '**Marliacea Albida**' As with all water lilies, plant in still water in full sun. Planting depth 1¹/₂ft/45cm

Nymphaea '**Marliacea Chromatella**' Flowers of deep, buttery yellow. Planting depth 1¹/₂ft/45cm

Fill attractive pots and containers on a
seasonal basis. Here the early-flowering *Iris
reticulata* will bring cheer to the cold days of
late winter.

Through the Seasons

The owner of any small garden must endeavor to sustain interest the whole year round. This is not, it must be admitted, always easy to achieve. But it can be done. It requires a sound knowledge of plants, skill in their arrangement, effective husbandry, a critical eye and close attention to detail. It demands patience, a flexible approach, imagination, good judgement and common sense. That said, the results will amply repay the time and effort spent.

Key trees, shrubs and perennials will all play a part. They will be those which, for whatever reason, contribute to the overall garden scene in more than a single way. It may be that they fruit as well as flower, or that interesting foliage turns color later on, or that bark takes on a prominence in winter. It could be no more than the effect of frost on an evergreen or the continuous flowering of a perennial. What matters, in a small space, is to consider carefully the merits of all plants chosen for the garden.

Erica carnea 'Myretoun Ruby' Winter–flowering heathers will bloom continuously during the winter and early spring. E, 1 × 1¹/₂ft/30 × 45cm

Bergenia purpurascens These handsome leaves are in their winter livery. As the days warm they will revert to green. E, 1 × 1¹/₂ft/30 × 45cm

***Hedera helix* 'Cristata'** Include this restrained ivy for its very prettily shaped leaves. E, 9ft/2.7m

***Hedera helix* 'Buttercup'** Such intensity of color is especially effective out of season. E, 9ft/2.7m

***Hedera helix* 'Glacier'** Ivies make an effective ground cover in a position of semi-shade. E, 9ft/2.7m

***Hedera helix* 'Goldheart'** will provide a splash of welcome color all through the year. E, 9ft/2.7m

***Ilex aquifolium* 'Ferox Argentea'** All the evergreen hollies, and this one is no exception, make for interesting backdrops. E, 8 × 8ft/2.4 × 2.4m

Acer shirasawanum aureum A golden-leafed Japanese maple to act as a beacon from spring until the fall. ◑, 10 × 8ft/ 3 × 2.4m

***Aucuba japonica* 'Gold Dust'** will produce a succession of red berries from the fall through to the spring. E, 8 × 8ft/2.4 × 2.4m

Artemisia **'Powis Castle'** A perfect foil for pale pinks, blues and rich purples. ○, E, 3 × 4ft/1 × 1.2m

Euonymus fortunei **'Silver Queen'** Another shrub tolerant of some shade. E, 3 × 5ft/1 × 1.5m

Hebe pinguifolia **'Pagei'** Grey-green leaves, which remain attractive all year. E, 1 × 3ft/30cm × 1m

Helictotrichon sempervirens Slender blue-grey leaves are attractive at all times. Cut to the ground each spring. ○, 4 × 1ft/1.2m × 30cm

Festuca ovina Grasses all contribute year-round interest. ○, 10in × 1ft/25 × 30cm

Stachys byzantina For most of the year grey, woolly lamb's ears form an effective carpet. ○, E, 1¹/₂ × 1ft/45 × 30cm

Ballota pseudodictamnus is best positioned in sun on well drained soil. ○, E, 1 × 1¹/₂ft/30 × 45cm

Abelia schumanii Warm flowers of mauve-pink are produced from summer into the fall. Semi-E, 5 × 5ft/1.5 × 1.5m

Indigofera heterantha A long flowering season, from midsummer through to the fall. ○, 6 × 6ft/2 × 2m

***Euphorbia dulcis* 'Chameleon'** Purple foliage gradually changes through green to orange-red. 16 × 16in/40 × 40cm

***Allium schoenoprasum* 'Forescate'** Pink flowered chives make an attractive edging plant. 1 × 1ft/30 × 30cm

Clematis **'Dr. Ruppel'** will flower freely throughout the summer. Height depends on soil and situation.

Rosa **'Cornelia'** This hybrid musk rose will flower all summer and is ideal for a mixed border. ○, 4 × 4ft/1.2 × 1.2m

Lavatera **'Barnsley'** will reward with a profusion of pale pink flowers for several months in summer. ○, 6 × 3ft/2 × 1m

Escallonia 'Iveyi' White flowers in mid to late summer are easily teamed with a contrasting clematis. E, 13 × 10ft/4 × 3m

Hydrangea quercifolia These white flower panicles which appear mid-summer will in time turn pink as the leaves color.
6 × 8ft/2 × 2.4m

Leucothöe fontanesiana Racemes of tiny white flowers appear in mid/late spring.
E, 5 × 10ft/1.5 × 3m

***Epimedium × youngianum* 'Niveum'**
After the delicate white spring flowers, prettily shaped leaves develop.
10in × 1ft/25 × 30cm

Pittosporum tenuifolium Highly ornamental, evergreen shrub which is much favored by flower arrangers. Plant away from cold winds in a sheltered, sunny site. E, 16 × 13ft/5 × 4m

Clematis armandii Particularly welcome in the early spring for its wonderfully scented flowers. ○, E, height depends on soil and situation.

Eryngium tripartitum Steely-blue flowers throughout the mid-summer. ○, 1½ft × 10in/45 × 25cm

Helleborus foetidus **'Wester Flisk'** This variety has grey-green leaves supported by red-tinged flower stalks in late winter/early spring. ◑, E, 1¹/₂ × 1¹/₂ft/45 × 45cm

Rosa **'Graham Thomas'** A new English rose which may be relied upon to bloom summer and fall. ○, 5 × 3ft/1.5 × 1m

Erysimum **'Bowles' Mauve'** This perennial wallflower is in bloom for virtually every month of the year. 2 × 2ft/60 × 60cm

242

Pulsatilla vulgaris Pasque flowers, also in white and wine red, are charming in flower in the spring. 1 × 1ft/30 × 30cm

***Salvia officinalis* 'Purpurascens'** Leaves act as a foil to other plantings throughout the entire year. O, E, 2 × 3ft/60cm × 1m

***Clematis* 'Lord Nevill'** Intense blue flowers during the early summer and in the fall. Height depends on soil and situation.

Viola labradorica Dark leafed foliage is near evergreen; tiny flowers of lilac, mauve and purple in spring and summer. 4in × 1ft/10 × 30cm

Viburnum davidii A low-growing, spreading shrub which will thrive in awkward places. E, 3 × 5ft/90cm × 1.5m

***Viburnum tinus* 'Eve Price'** Easy to grow, the pink flowers appear from the fall until spring. E, 8 × 8ft/2.4 × 2.4m

Cotoneaster horizontalis In maturity this shrub develops an exciting framework. Rich fall leaf color combines with scarlet berries. 5 × 5ft/1.5 × 1.5m

The simplicity of this variegated holly
surrounded by box balls is wholly matched in
style and sophistication.

Index

Aquilegia hybrids

Dicentra 'Langtrees'

Spiral bay tree (*Laurus nobilis*) in lavender bed.

Peonies with yellow *Achillea* and mauve *Nepeta*

Acknowledgements

Many of the photographs were taken in the author's garden, Arrow Cottage, Ledgemoor, Weobley, Herefordshire. The producers would also like to thank the many people and organizations who have allowed photographs to be taken for this book, including the following:

Mr and Mrs Terence Aggett; Pelham Aldrich-Blake, Bristol (pages 96–103, designed by Julian Dowle of The Julian Dowle Partnership, The Old Malt House, High Street, Newent, Gloucestershire GL18 1AY); Anthony and Fenja Anderson; Aspects Garden Design; Mr and Mrs A Bambridge, Llanvair Kilgeddin, Abergavenny; Barnsley House, Barnsley, Cirencester; Prue Bellak (pages 74–77); Lindsay Bousfield, Acton Beauchamp Roses, Worcester; Bromesberrow Place Nurseries, Ledbury; Burford House, Tenbury Wells; David and Mary Butler; Chilcombe House, Chilcombe; Mrs B Cope; Dr Lallie Cox, Woodpeckers, Marlcliff, Bidford-on-Avon; Croft Castle, (National Trust); Kim Davies, Lingen; Dinmore Manor, Hereford; Richard Edwards, Well Cottage, Blakemere; Mr and Mrs J Hepworth, Elton Hall, Wigmore; Jacquie Gordon, Garden Design, 'Rattys', Glebe Road, Newent, Gloucestershire GL18 1BJ (pages 78–81); Mr and Mrs R Humphries; Kim Hurst, The Cottage Herbery, Boraston, Tenbury Wells; Mr and Mrs J James; Kiftsgate Court, near Chipping Camden; Mr and Mrs D Lewis, Ash Farm, Much Birch; Mirabel Osler (pages 62–67); The Picton Garden, Colwall; Mrs Richard Paice, Bourton House; Anthony Poulton and Brian Stenlake, 21 Swinton Lane, Worcester (pages 82–87); Mr and Mrs D Pritchard, Newbury (pages 116–119); RHS Garden, Wisley; Mr and Mrs Charles Reading, Hereford (pages 68–73); Mrs Clive Richards, Lower Hope, Ullingswick; Tony and Caroline Ridler, 7 Saint Peter's Terrace, Cockett, Swansea SA2 0FW (pages 108–115); Mary Ann Robinson; Paul and Betty Smith, The Old Chapel, Ludlow (pages 88–91); Malley Terry; Raymond Treasure, Stockton Bury Farm, Kimbolton; Mr and Mrs P Trevor-Jones, Preen Manor, Shropshire; Carole and Shelby Tucker; Wakehurst Place (National Trust); Richard Walker; Mr and Mrs D Williams–Thomas, The Manor House, Birlingham.

The summerhouse in Mirabel Osler's garden on page 67 was made by Richard Craven, Stoke St Milborough, Shropshire SY8 2EJ.

The photograph of the gold-medal Preferred Direct Garden at Chelsea 1997 (designed by Jacquie Gordon and Julian Dowle of The Julian Dowle Partnership) on pages 12–13 is by Derek Harris.